Black Muslim Refugee

Black Muslim Refugee

MILITARISM, POLICING, AND SOMALI AMERICAN RESISTANCE TO STATE VIOLENCE

Maxamed Abumaye

UNIVERSITY OF CALIFORNIA PRESS

University of California Press
Oakland, California

© 2025 by Maxamed Abumaye

All rights reserved.

Cataloging-in-Publication data is on file at the Library of Congress.

ISBN 978-0-520-35631-3 (cloth : alk. paper)
ISBN 978-0-520-35632-0 (pbk. : alk. paper)
ISBN 978-0-520-97608-5 (ebook)

Manufactured in the United States of America

GPSR Authorized Representative: Easy Access System Europe, Mustamäe tee 50, 10621 Tallinn, Estonia, gpsr.requests@easproject.com

34 33 32 31 30 29 28 27 26 25
10 9 8 7 6 5 4 3 2 1

Contents

Introduction *1*

1 US Imperialism and Somali Refugees *22*

2 The Carceral Refugee Camp *48*

3 Confronting Anti-Black Racism: Militarized Policing in San Diego *68*

4 Somali Refugees and the War on Terror *100*

Conclusion: Somali Refugee Youths and Black Freedom, Summer 2020 *141*

Notes *151*
Bibliography *179*
Index *191*

Introduction

Twin Pandemics

I wrote the introduction for *Black Muslim Refugee: Militarism, Policing, and Somali American Resistance to State Violence* during the summer of 2020, amid the devastating impact that COVID-19 and police violence inflicted on Black people throughout the country. According to an ACLU report on police shootings, in 2020, 24 percent of fatal police shootings resulted in the death of a Black person.[1] And as of June 2023, 156,074 Black people had died due to COVID-19.[2] Tari Ajadi and Debrah Thompson call COVID-19 and police shootings "twin pandemics": "We cannot think of these two phenomena—anti-Black racism and COVID-19—as separate. Both are global, though nationally textured. Both had the potential to be mitigated by decisive government action or accelerated by epic government failure. But the two pandemics are not just similar, they are interlocking, and have wrought havoc on racialized communities across the continent."[3]

Christina Sharpe illustrates how Black lives are replete with violence and negation; to be Black is to live with the specter of death. Sharpe defines "the wake" as "a new analytic, as the wake

[1]

and wake work" to plot, map, and collect "the archives of the everyday of Black immanent and imminent death, and in tracking the ways we resist, rupture, and disrupt that immanence and imminence aesthetically and materially."[4] The Black Lives Matter protests that took place in the summer of 2020 encapsulated resistance to this immanence of Black death. Building on Sharpe's call to engage in "wake work," this book shows how Somali refugees resist and build lives in the context of both local and global US state violence.

My lived experiences as a Somali refugee and Black man in San Diego, California, directly intersected with the twin pandemics of COVID-19 and police violence directed at Black communities. That summer, I had contracted the COVID-19 virus and was also pulled over in El Cajon, San Diego, and experienced racial profiling at the hands of the police. The officer who pulled me over immediately asked, "Do you have a criminal record?" I wondered to myself if he asked this question to everyone he pulls over. His question was rooted in the assumption of my criminality, a racial logic in the United States that identifies criminality with Blackness.[5] These two experiences inspired me to join a series of Black Lives Matter protests in San Diego, which were led primarily by Somali refugee youths. It was a hot summer day when I first witnessed Somali youths with bullhorns in hand leading an animated crowd of people. The protest took place in La Mesa, San Diego, on May 30, 2020, with close to eight hundred people in attendance.[6] I was struck and moved by the fearlessness displayed by young Somali refugees as they confronted police to demand racial justice and police abolition.

This book is inspired by the Somali refugee youths' fervor and commitment to racial justice. Scholarship on the Black Lives Matter movement rarely centers Black refugees as leaders and activists. I privilege Black refugee stories as a means to highlight mobility and immobility as central issues that impact Black communities in the United States. Black refugees also bring to light the role of US militarism in subjecting Black people, globally and locally, to state violence.

We Are Here Because You Were There

This project, the first of its kind, exposes the links between US military violence abroad and police violence at home by focusing on Somali refugee narratives that detail this militarized violence. This multisited project traces Somali refugees' experiences with state violence from the Somali civil war to the Dadaab refugee camp in Kenya to their eventual arrival to San Diego. I argue that Somali refugees first encountered US militarism in Somalia during the 1992 US military invasion of Somalia, dubbed "Operation Restore Hope."[7] In other words, US militarism exacerbated the Somali refugee crises and continues to structure Somali refugee life in the United States. As such, the Somali refugee experience in the United States cannot be extricated from the Somali civil war that led to the exodus of millions of Somalis from their homelands.

In the United States, the relationship between US militarism and Somali refugees is often obscured in favor of depictions of the United States as a humanitarian nation. In showing that Somali refugees' arrival in San Diego was influenced by the 1992 US military invasion of Somalia, I disrupt the narrative that the United States rescues Somalis from violence by showing that the United States participated in the violence that led to the war.[8]

As a project that draws from the methodologies and theoretical framework of Critical Refugee Studies, this book considers refugees not as an object of study but as an analytic that exposes the often-hidden operations of US militarism. I follow the movement of Somali refugees from Somalia to Kenya to their eventual arrival in San Diego to reveal how US militarism structures Somali refugee life. I posit that a Somali refugee epistemology, constructed through storytelling, exposes the links between US militarism abroad and policing domestically.

From Somalia to Kenya to San Diego: My Story

Despite popular conceptions that refugees come to the United States directly from their home countries, most refugees spend time in a neighboring country before being resettled in the United States. For Somali refugees, that neighboring country is Kenya.[9] In 1991, during the height of the Somali civil war, hundreds of thousands of Somali refugees fled to Dadaab, Kenya.[10] In 1996, when I was five years old, my family of fifteen, which included my grandparents, aunts, and uncles, fled Somalia at the height of the civil war. My family did not want to leave Somalia but had to leave under the threat of unrelenting violence. It was a painful decision to leave Mogadishu, a city my family had lived in for generations. I vividly recollect leaving my childhood home, not once imagining that I would never see it again.

The horrors that we experienced along our path from Mogadishu to the Dadaab refugee camp in Kenya have stayed with me. We arrived at the refugee camp with nothing but the clothes on our backs. Ours was an experience shared by the other ninety thousand Somali refugees who left their homes in the early 1990s hoping to reach safety.[11] Once in Dadaab, we were immediately instructed to wait in one line to process paperwork and then promptly moved to another line to get food rations. This experience marked our first introduction to the intricate and cumbersome bureaucracy of the refugee camp.

Somali refugees routinely spend a decade in refugee camps, often with little hope for resettlement. According to the United Nations High Commissioner for Refugees, 78 percent of all refugees worldwide endure this protracted situation; only 3 percent of refugees ever get resettled.[12] The Dadaab refugee camp was constructed as a temporary shelter, designed to house only 90,000 refugees.[13] As of July 2020, there are 218,873 refugees in Dadaab, which underscores the cramped conditions that refugees live in.[14] Thus, for 200,000 Somali refugees, Dadaab has become not a temporary stop on the way to a final destination but rather a semi-permanent home. Many of these Somali families have now been in Dadaab for several generations. In the US news media, Somali refugees are invariably described as one-dimensional victims who are either in need of rescue or who are terrorist threats the state deems suspicious.[15] Yet the people I met in the refugee camps were engaged in collective world-making practices through art, poetry, and storytelling. I vividly remember my aunt reciting poetry and my mother teaching us about Somali folktales, all in the context of our confinement in the refugee camp. Even though our bodies were contained in the refugee camp, our imagination knew no bounds. Somali refugees brought these life-sustaining practices to the United States by building community centers, using their own apartments to shelter new Somali refugees, and continuing the practice of storytelling in the diaspora. I call these life-sustaining practices the "refugee repertoire"—a term coined by scholar Long Bui. Long defines the refugee repertoire "as the aesthetics and arts produced by refugees and their children."[16] I add to Long's analysis by arguing that refugee art, poetry, and storytelling are life-affirming practices that sustain Somali refugees through the trauma of war and displacement. Therefore, I focus on how Somali refugees bring these refugee repertoires developed in the refugee camp to San Diego. In my own family, for example, my mother has helped Somali refugee women win a dispute over a racist landlord, and my father helps members of the Somali refugee community in the United States navigate the intricate bureaucracy of the US immigration system.

The United States became a top destination for Somali refugees who were able to achieve resettlement. My family was granted resettlement to the United States in 1996. Although it has been several decades since I left Dadaab, I still remember the tree on which the list of those who were selected for resettlement was posted. As a child in the refugee camp, I would go to this tree every day hoping to see my family's name on the list. I recollect the jubilation I felt when I finally saw our name and discovered that the United States would be our destination. The United States was assigned to us because my father could speak English and act as a translator for other Somali refugees. My father learned English during the four years he spent as a university student in Germany during the late 1970s. Our choices were either to migrate to the United States, a country few of us had ever seen outside of the TV screen, or continue living in perpetuity in the refugee camp. My family chose to brave the unknown. In June 1996, we arrived in Wheaton, Illinois, as the *first* Somali refugee family in the state. To commemorate this moment, a newspaper reporter came and interviewed my mother and father about their experiences. Years later, in 2011, I came to San Diego for graduate school hoping to find ways of understanding the Somali civil war and my family's turbulent trajectory from

Somalia to the United States. Yet in the San Diego Somali refugee community, I was struck by the resilience and creativity of Somali refugees as they rebuilt their lives and sustained each other by sharing their time, homes, and energy with newly arrived Somali refugees. The determination and experiences of the Somali refugee community in San Diego mirrored that of my own family.[17]

San Diego: Militarism and Policing

The Militarized Refuge

In the early 1990s, one thousand Somali refugees set off from the Dadaab refugee camp to San Diego,[18] an established destination for refugees due to the existence of four refugee resettlement agencies and several rooted immigrant communities.[19] The presence of refugees in San Diego dates back to the late 1970s, when hundreds of thousands of Southeast Asians landed at Camp Pendleton in North County, San Diego, for resettlement. Many stayed in the county, helping make San Diego a beacon for displaced people.[20] Sociologists Linda Borgen and Rubén Rumbuat argue that "the selection of the Marine Corps' Camp Pendleton as one of four main camps for the resettlement of Vietnamese refugees who fled after the fall of Saigon in 1975 helped make San Diego one of the principal areas of Vietnamese as well as Cambodian, Lao, and Hmong refugee resettlement in the country, peaking during the 1980s."[21] Borgen and Rumbuat's analysis shows that San Diego's refugee community has historically been shaped by US militarism.

Data provided by the US Department of State shows that California resettles more refugees than any other state in the country.[22] A large portion of refugees were resettled in City Heights, San

Diego, because "destination cities for refugees are assigned cases based upon several factors, with the most important considerations being presence of the same or closely related ethnic communities, the strength of the nonprofit service sector for refugees, and the availability of affordable housing and gainful employment," according to Ethnic Studies scholar Jesse Mills.[23] City Heights fits the criteria as a destination city based on the guidelines set forth by the US Office of Refugee Resettlement, which is responsible for resettling newly arrived refugees.[24]

In San Diego, Somali refugees once again encountered the US military, as San Diego is home to six military bases, including those of the Marines, Navy, and Coast Guard.[25] Historian Abraham Shragge argues that after World War I, "San Diego's civic leaders and citizens took a series of steps which just as rapidly turned the city into a major metropolitan-military complex." Therefore, San Diego "identified itself as a complete 'navy town,' where the needs, interests and desires of the service seemed always to come first."[26]

As a militarized city as well the largest refugee-receiving county in the state of California, San Diego embodies the relationship between militarism and refugees. Indeed, three of the largest refugee groups in San Diego—Vietnamese, Somalis, and Iraqis—were displaced by US wars in their respective countries: Vietnam (1962–73), Somalia (1992–94), and Iraq (2003–11).[27] Interestingly, the earliest Somali refugees to arrive in San Diego were a small group of Somali soldiers training with American troops at Camp Pendleton—yet another link between Somalis in San Diego and US militarism. By the time Somali refugees began moving in large numbers to the United States in the 1990s, San Diego had two of the major prerequisites for refugee placement: cultural and social ties and a robust network of refugee resettlement services.

When I relocated to San Diego, I met members of the Somali refugee community whose experiences mirrored my own. In 2012, I joined the Somali Youth League (SYL), a San Diego-based Somali activist organization that mobilized the Somali community. Through my work with the SYL, I came to see that *militarism* and *policing* profoundly impacted the lived experiences of the Somali refugee community in San Diego. Tracing the militarization and policing of Somali lives became the focus of my research and activism ever since.

Police Militarization

San Diego is a militarized city that underscores the national trend of police militarization, which has been exacerbated by the War on Drugs and the War on Terror. As I will document in this book, Somali refugees, as Black Muslims, have consistently, often viscerally, encountered the intersections between these two wars. Sumeya, a Somali refugee residing in City Heights, describes the cumulative and violent impact of the War on Drugs and the War on Terror on the Somali refugee community: "When we first came to San Diego in 1993, the police were always attacking us because we are Black, and arresting Somalis for no reason. Now the police harass us because we are Muslim ... they attack our families in Somalia, my brother in Somalia tells me he hears American bombs dropped in Mogadishu every night."[28] For refugees like Sumeya, there is a direct connection between domestic police violence against Black communities in San Diego and US military violence against Black people in Somalia. This form of knowing represents a Somali refugee epistemology that exposes the scope and reach of US state violence.

For their part, state and federal agencies utilize scholarship from the field of terrorism studies to surveil Muslim communities. According to the FBI's Joint Terrorism Task Force (JTTF), Somali refugees represent an internal terrorist threat that needs to be policed and surveilled. Al-Shabaab is a terrorist organization that emerged in Somalia in 2006 and has been the target of US counterterrorism in Somalia and within the Somali diaspora. Moreover, US state agencies such as the FBI use the argument that Al-Shabaab recruits Somali youths in the United States to justify surveilling the Somali refugee community in San Diego. In short, the US global War on Terror marks Somali refugees as terrorist threats in Somalia and San Diego. In 2009, the San Diego Police Department (SDPD) created a counterterrorism division tasked specifically with surveilling the Somali refugee community.[29] Moreover, San Diego is home to a joint counterterrorism taskforce that has been known to harass and racially profile the Somali refugee community.[30] Somali refugees experience surveillance from the police because Somalis are Black and Muslim, and they navigate the state violence that operates at the intersections of anti-Black racism and Islamophobia. The FBI's JTTF partnered with the SDPD to surveil the Somali refugee community.[31] San Diego's wealth, proximity to the US-Mexico border, and heavy military presence makes it a key site for the development and testing of surveillance technologies. In 2017, the SDPD coordinated with the JTTF to install security cameras on three thousand streetlights throughout San Diego, which were used by the police during the Black Lives Matter protests in the summer of 2020 to identify protesters.[32] As I will show, police have taken on the work of counterterrorism, utilizing the discourse of Islamophobia to justify targeting Muslim communities. As a response to militarized policing, young Somali activists in San

Diego have condemned the over-policing in their communities. A local Somali activist named Hodan shared how the militarization of the police in San Diego made her feel:

> The militarized way that policing is done in the United States, one of the most militarized countries in the world. I am not talking about just from a militaristic perspective, I'm talking about all the way down to your local police, it impacts your psyche. It impacts and affects the way you move, the way you show up. I mean, people have this sort of anxiety. There's a sense of fear that kind of comes from it, or a sense of anxiety, or a sense of like, you know what, I'm just going to be profiled.[33]

Although the presence of militarized policing in San Diego instills fear in Somali refugees who have long been targets of US militarized violence, this fear has not stopped Somali refugee youths from finding ways both overt and subtle to resist state violence.

By conducting a nine-year ethnography of Somali refugees in San Diego, I learned that the impetus for Somali youth activism during the summer of 2020 was their parents' unwavering determination to survive in the context of a brutal civil war, an inhumane refugee camp, and over-policing in the inner city. Aisha, a Somali activist in the Black Lives Matter movement, credits her mother:

> I think the power of a mother, right, and the love and the fierce love of a mother for her child. She's my best friend and the person that I owe so much of my thinking, and my like wanting to make the world a better place, you know, for her. Everything that I do she's proud of me and she's my number one supporter and she believes

in the power of this work even though she doesn't have time for it, because she's surviving and she's, you know, working three jobs and doing a lot.[34]

In each of these spaces—Somalia, Dadaab, and City Heights—Somali refugees employed community building as an essential tool for survival and resistance. In the absence of state resources and protections, Somali refugees found ways to feed, shelter, and protect each other from the neglect and violence of the state. Young Somali refugees in San Diego have taken on the same ethos and are building community with Syrian refugees, Central American refugees, Mexican immigrants, working-class African American communities, and Southeast Asian immigrants to challenge the militarized carceral state. The Somali refugee experience with state violence shows the ways that the military and police join forces to inflict violence on communities of color and the collective methods of resistance to militarism in the communities that are its targets. Young Somali refugee activists are engaging in the act of world-making by advocating for the abolition of both the police and the military.

The Black Muslim Refugee

According to a Pew Research Center analysis of US Census Bureau data, the foreign-born segment has played an important role in the diversity and growth of the Black population of the United States over the past four decades. In 2019, one in ten Black people in the United States were immigrants. Africa has accounted for the fastest growth in the Black immigrant population; the number of Black immigrants from Africa more than tripled from 2000 to 2019.[35]

African immigration to the United States grew after the passage of the Immigration and Naturalization Act of 1965, which eliminated racial quotas for immigration admissions. From 1965 to the early 1990s, most African immigrants came to the United States to pursue higher education.[36] In the early 1990s, African refugees began to arrive in large numbers due to a series of wars on the African continent. According to data from the Migration Policy Institute, "More than 75 percent of the African foreign born in the United States have arrived since 1990."[37]

Somali refugees represent a Black immigrant community whose presence in the United States is not directly due to transatlantic slavery but to US imperialism and militarism in Africa. In the United States, various scholars have argued that transatlantic slavery is the origin of Blackness and the structures that continue to condition Black life writ large.[38] Black Studies scholar Michelle Wright also argues that, "as recent anthologies such as *The Other African Americans* show, many Western nations are now (and in many cases have been since the postwar era) receiving Black African immigrants whose histories, while certainly tied to Atlantic slavery, more often narrate themselves through colonialism or postwar socioeconomic changes than through the Middle Passage."[39]

While foundational to US Black Studies, rooting Blackness in transatlantic slavery often elides how US imperialism and colonialism continue to produce the dispersal of Black people. My work contributes to the field of Black Diaspora Studies by highlighting the role of US imperialism in producing the dispersal of Black people and how it continues to structure and delimit contemporary Black life. As Roderick Ferguson posits, "International black migrations demand that we decenter African American history as the origin of African American racial formations and as the purpose of African American studies."⁴⁰ The growing presence of African immigrants in the United States brings to the fore the significance of US imperialism in shaping contemporary Black life in the United States and in the global Black diaspora. By focusing on the experiences of Somali refugees with US militarism this work highlights the impacts of US militarism on Black life.

This book also complicates Muslimness and the discourse of Islamophobia by examining the experiences of Black Muslims such as Somali refugees. Discourses on Islamophobia and its impacts on Muslim communities routinely focus on Arab and South Asian Muslims with little attention paid to Black Muslims.⁴¹ In her book *Muslim Cool*, Su'ad Abdul Khabeer argues that "Muslims have a long history in the United States, beginning with the involuntary migration of enslaved African Muslims."⁴² Therefore, the presence of Black Muslims in the United States long predates the arrival of Somali refugees. Black Muslims account for 21 percent of the Muslim population, according to data from the Pew Research Center.⁴³

Because Somali refugees are rendered invisible in narratives regarding state violence against Muslim people and Black people, Somali refugees experience multiple erasures in the United States. As a result, young Somali activists have had to organize in Black spaces, Muslim spaces, and immigrant spaces to articulate the need for an intersectional movement against state violence. Drawing inspiration from the activism of Somali refugee youths, I investigate the relationship between anti-Blackness and Islamophobia to highlight the intersections of racial discourses and the communities most impacted by them. Muriam Haleh Davis examines how anti-Black racism and Islamophobia are viewed as incommensurable in the United States, where "a particular anti-racist commitment rooted in ontological approaches to race also highlights the political dangers of placing discussions of Islamophobia alongside anti-Black racism. Scholars who espouse Afropessimist approaches, such as Frank B. Wilderson III, view Blackness as coterminous with slavery and social death, arguing that anti-Blackness cannot be analogous to other forms of racism."[44] Whereas Wilderson posits that "the black subject, the slave, is vital to civil society's political economy," thereby framing Blackness within the analytics of slavery.[45] The Somali subject position asks: Can Blackness exist outside the context of slavery and its aftermaths? What is the role of colonialism and imperialism in shaping Black subjectivity? How has Islamophobia structured Black experiences with state violence? I answer these questions by centering the narratives and stories of Somali refugees as they navigated the terrain of anti-Black racism and Islamophobia.

An interview I conducted with Somali activist Suada Nur in San Diego revealed the difficulties of navigating state violence as a Black Muslim: "And people don't realize that, you know, when you get stopped by a cop, he doesn't ask, 'What type of black are you?' Black is black. You're going to be impacted by it, right? And then there's that double effect of being Black and then also being Muslim."[46] Somali refugees bring this experiential knowledge of anti-Black racism and Islamophobia to the Black Lives Matter movement by making visible the relationship between police murders of Black people and US drone strikes in Somalia. Somali refugees expose the violence the US military inflicts on Black people globally, thereby enriching the conversations on Black people's experiences with and resistance to state violence. Donna Auston captures the Black Muslim experience when she states, "They are Black in a world rife with anti-Black racism; they are Muslim in an age of rampant Islamophobia."[47] This project demonstrates what can we learn about policing, militarism, and the clandestine operation of the FBI during the War on Terror if we take seriously the experiential knowledge of Somali refugees who are not merely objects of state violence but are subjects of knowledge who do the work of exposing and challenging this state violence.

Carceral Militarism

The field of carceral studies has produced generative works that link prisons and police to the afterlife of slavery. Scholars such as Dylan Rodriguez, Khalil Gibran Muhammad, Michelle Alexander, and Ruth Wilson Gilmore highlight how the carceral state is an extension of the racial logics of slavery and Jim Crow, which reduce Blackness to criminality and captivity.[48] On the other hand, scholarship on US militarism has exposed that the United States is an empire in a constant state of war, thereby showing that US empire is defined by war. Moreover, scholars such as Yến Lê Espiritu and Simeon Man have shown how racial narratives of othering are central to US wars abroad.[49] Whereas policing in the United States is conditioned by the legacy of slavery and Jim Crow as racial projects linking Blackness to criminality. These two fields—carceral studies and militarism studies—rarely enter into conversation with each other. My use of the term "carceral militarism" is intended to draw insights from both these fields and to bring them into conversation to demonstrate that policing in the United States is also conditioned by US militarism abroad.

The Black Muslim refugee subject therefore exposes the compounding impacts of militarism and policing in Black communities. Moreover, Black Muslim refugees are rendered mute in the news narratives of police violence against Black people and US military violence against Muslims. An example of this erasure is a *Time* article by Sanya Mansoor titled "'At the Intersection of Two Criminalized Identities': Black and Non-Black Muslims Confront a Complicated Relationship with Policing and Anti-Blackness."[50] This article cites the two criminalized identities of Blackness and Muslimness but fails to imagine that Black Muslims exist and navigate life at the intersections of these two identities. I highlight the relationship between anti-Blackness and Islamophobia by illuminating how police deploy Islamophobia and how the US military deploys anti-Black racism through an analysis of the US military's 1992 "Operation Restore Hope" and the SDPD's Joint Counterterrorism Task Force.

Consequently, the Black Muslim refugee subject highlights how racial discourses intersect to produce militarized police violence. Moreover, the racial discourses that link Blackness to criminality and Muslimness to terrorism intersect to shape the lived experiences of Somali refugees. This book also brings Critical Refugee Studies to Black Studies by interrogating the violence US militarism inflicts on Black people through militarized policing in the United States and drone strikes in Somalia. Moreover, by bringing Critical Refugee Studies to Black Studies, I show that Black refugee life is not only conditioned by the legacy of slavery but also by US imperialism. I juxtapose Black people's experiences with militarized violence in East Africa to Black people's encounters with militarized policing in San Diego to illuminate the global circuits of US militarism and its impact on Black refugee life. Therefore, state violence against Black people is not limited to the United States but operates on a global scale.

As I will elaborate, Somali refugees move from the militarized space of the Somali civil war to the carceral space of the refugee camp. Somali refugees' experience with militarism in Somalia and carcerality in Kenya provides the basis for a refugee epistemology of carceral militarism. My analytic of carceral militarism also exposes the increasing presence of militarized policing in the United States. Through an analysis of the SDPD's deployment of militarized SWAT teams in San Diego during the early 1990s, I developed the term carceral militarism to explore the interstice between the US police and military. Carceral militarism conjoins Ruth Wilson Gilmore's definition of the carceral state, as a state that profits from the incarceration of its marginalized populace, with Yến Lê Espiritu's idea of "militarized refuge(es)"—that "refuge and refugees are co-constitutive, and that both are the (by) product of US militarism."[51] Carceral militarism as an analytic brings to light the trend of police militarization and its impact on refugee communities. Moreover, carceral militarism underscores the increasing threat of militarism and policing to the lives of Black people both globally and domestically. Therefore, this project elucidates the global and local militarization of Black life. What can we learn about the militarization of the police by centering on the experiences of Somali refugees? I answer these questions by foregrounding Somali refugee experiences with and resistance to militarized policing in the United States and US military violence in Somalia.

This book also provides an analysis of resistance to state violence. Somali refugee encounters with US military intervention in Somalia and the militarized policing in San Diego expose the often hidden yet violent operations of carceral militarism as a strategy of US empire, at home and abroad. In looking at these encounters, I am interested in the tools and strategies that Somali refugees have developed to navigate their lives in transit, in the refugee camp and in San Diego. I juxtapose a discourse analysis of US military, police, and FBI training manuals and memos with an ethnography of the Somali refugee community to read these documents differently. I challenge the dominant racial narrative about Somali refugees produced in these official documents with the counternarratives produced by Somali refugees. In these documents, the state and its agents claim that Somalis are terrorists and criminals, whereas the Somali refugees I interview argue the state is criminal and a source of terror in their lives. I critique the state narratives that construct Somali refugees as inherently violent and needing to be met with violence by exposing the violence of the state. Throughout this manuscript, I use pseudonyms to protect the anonymity of the Somali refugees I interviewed.

Due to my positionality as a refugee and as a scholar, I also employ autoethnography to interweave my personal narrative with the structural forces of militarism and policing that profoundly shape the lives of Somali refugees. Autoethnography is a foundational methodology for Critical Refugee Studies because CRS challenges the framing of refugees as objects of study and considers refugees as subjects of knowledge. CRS argues that refugee experiences are not merely data but rather ways of seeing the world.

Overview

I structure the four chapters in this book in accordance with the route Somali refugees take from Somalia to San Diego—one that mirrors my own family's journey—in order to link US militarism in Somalia with police violence in City Heights, San Diego. This route highlights the carceral militarism that shapes the lives of so many Somali refugees. Somali refugees' journey across the oceans highlights the increasingly carceral and militarized spaces that Somali refugees occupy. I argue that the movement of Somali refugees along this route—through the carceral and militarized spaces of Somali, Kenya, and San Diego—reveals the transnational circuits of US militarism. I foreground Somali refugee stories as forms of knowledge that provide critical insights into the workings of US militarism abroad and domestically through militarized police.

Chapter 1 investigates the origins of US militarism in Somalia with the culmination of the Somali civil war, which conditioned the Somali refugee exodus. I interrogate the role of US militarism in creating the conditions of possibility for the Somali civil war that catapulted millions of Somali refugees from their homeland. In the second chapter, I illuminate the experiences of Somali refugees in the Dadaab refugee camp. The Somali refugee community did not arrive to San Diego in a vacuum; many spent years living in refugee camps in Kenya. Chapter 2 follows Somali refugees after they fled civil strife in their own country only to encounter the carceral space of the Dadaab refugee camp in Kenya. The refugee camp formed a carceral space organized around technologies of policing and surveillance used to govern Somali refugees; however, I will also show how Somali refugees employed counter-technologies to survive and even thrive in these carceral spaces. In chapter 3, I trace Somali refugees' arrival in City Heights, San Diego, from the Dadaab refugee camp and their experience with militarized policing. I analyze the continuity with which militarized policing follows Somali refugees from Kenya to San Diego. In the face of militarized policing, Somali refugees redeveloped, adapted, and further refined their tools of resistance to survive these multiple carceral and militarized spaces. Somali refugees did not only bring their trauma to the United States, they also brought tools and strategies to survive and resist state violence. One tool that emerged from the refugee camp is the collective pooling of resources among Somali refugees, a strategy that continues to be employed by Somali refugees in City Heights. Upon arriving to San Diego, Somali refugees helped each other with food, housing, transportation, and translation services.

In chapter 4, I highlight Somali refugees' experiences with the War on Terror, both abroad in Somalia and domestically in San Diego. I pay close attention to the state's deployment of Islamophobia as a means to racialize Somali refugees and mark them as terrorist threats. The refugee stories I document in this book reveal that the Black lives lost in Somalia are deeply intertwined with the Black lives lost in San Diego. I also utilize discourse analysis to interrogate FBI training manuals that racialize the Somali refugee community as a terrorist threat. The FBI primarily focuses on Somali refugee youths who they believe are vulnerable to radicalization. I examine the institutionalization of counterterrorism programs in San Diego that highlight how the police and US military coordinate with each other to surveil Somali refugees. I also interrogate the work of specialists in the field of terrorism studies to reveal the ways in which scholarly research can and does work on behalf of the state.

1 US Imperialism and Somali Refugees

Somali refugees didn't leave Somalia simply to find a better life in America; rather, Somali refugees fled the violence of a war that was shaped by the legacies of US imperialism in Somalia. In this chapter, I complicate the dominant narrative that the United States rescued Somali refugees from the Somali civil war by detailing the long history of US militarism in Somalia. Throughout this chapter, I juxtapose archival materials with oral histories of Somali refugees to interrogate the role of US imperialism in the Somali civil war. I trace the origin of US militarism in Somalia to map out its enduring impact on Somali refugee life in America. What do we learn about the Somali civil war and US militarism in Somalia if we place Somali refugees' lived experience at the center? Moreover, why are Somali refugees in the United States of all places? The answers to these questions can be derived from an analysis of US imperialism and its relationship to Somali refugees.

In 1993, then-president Bill Clinton delivered a speech justifying American military involvement in the Somali civil war. Clinton began the speech with this statement: "We started this mission for the right reasons and we're going to finish it in the right way. In a sense, we came to Somalia to rescue innocent people in a burning house. We've nearly put the fire out, but some smoldering embers remain. If we leave them now, those embers will reignite into flames and people will die again."[1] The burning house is an apt analogy for the series of historical events that led to the collapse of the Somali state and the subsequent flight of close to one million displaced Somali refugees.[2] Aisha, an elder in the Somali refugee community in San Diego and survivor of the war, refutes former President Clinton's claim, stating, "The US was not rescuing Somalis from the Somali civil war when they sent their military to Somalia because America is partly responsible for the Somali civil war."[3] How could the United States claim to save Somalis from a burning house if it had participated in setting the house on fire in the first place? I argue that US imperialism, along with British and Italian colonialism, played a key role in the Somali civil war. Moreover, I posit that US imperialism produced the Somali refugee diaspora in America. I will delve into an analysis of Somali history to contextualize this argument.

From Colonialism to Independence, 1884–1960

It was at the 1884 Berlin Conference that the British formalized their colonial relationship to Somalia. The conference was a historic meeting of European powers, where the borders of the African continent were drawn and codified. According to Wang Shih-tsung, "The Berlin Conference took place from 15 November 1884 to 26 February 1885 involving 14 countries—roughly all the states of Europe except Switzerland, along with Turkey and the United States—following intensified colonial rivalries in West Africa." The conference was "called by Bismarck in collaboration with the French Government . . . [and] held in the same rooms in which the Congress of 1878 sat."[4] The United States' presence at the Berlin Conference shows its early imperial interest in the African continent. The civilizing mission and the suppression of slavery emerged as key themes from this conference, as the document titled "General Act of the Berlin Conference on West Africa, 26 February 1885" shows: "All the Powers exercising sovereign rights or influence in the aforesaid territories bind themselves to watch over the preservation of the native tribes, and to care for the improvement of the conditions of their moral and material well-being."[5]

The Berlin Conference was convened to deter conflict between the various colonial powers over the occupation of African lands. Yet the resulting effect of the conference was the exploitation of African resources and labor, which contradicts the purported aim of the conference to maintain the "material well-being of native tribes."[6] Sumeya Hassan, a Somali refugee in San Diego, provides a thoughtful analysis of the Berlin conference: "The Europeans divided Somalia into three parts during the Berlin Conference like our nation was a piece of meat they could break apart and keep for themselves, but we are more than that."[7] Sumeya's metaphor highlights the objectification of Somalia and its people under colonialism while also centering the complex humanity of Somali people.

It was at this conference, with no African representatives present, that Europeans divided Somalia into three distinct regions. Britain partitioned off northern Somalia; Italy, southern Somalia; and France, northeast Somalia. As young Somali activist Ahmed cleverly states, "This is why Somalis drink tea in the morning and have spaghetti for dinner: we were colonized by both the British and Italians."[8] This demarcation of the boundaries of Somalia created decades of border conflict in East Africa.[9]

In 1946, the United States also became interested in Somalia because of its strategic location on the Indian Ocean. Influence over Somalia would allow the United States access to the profitable trade routes on the Indian Ocean. A British colonial document produced in 1946 signaled early signs of US imperial interest in Somalia:

> The international implications of a request for British trusteeship over any of the territories must thus be balanced against the strategic advantages which we would thereby acquire. Such a request would not obtain the support of the United States Government, since, as mentioned above, the American Secretary of State's Deputy in London has stated that they could not support a claim by any one of the Big Four to Individual Trusteeship over any of the Colonies. Trusteeship by one of the British Dominions would probably be regarded as a subterfuge of British imperialist interests and would equally not receive United States support.[10]

This document reveals the tensions between British and American imperial aspirations for Somalia. This memo marks the decline of British imperialism and the ascension of US imperialism in the twentieth century. The United States had very little contact with Somalia and its people until the twentieth century. Some of the first Somalis to travel to the United States were sailors, many of whom were involved in trade with New York in the 1920s.[11] Nasra, a Somali refugee living in San Diego, stated that "my great grandfather was a Somali sailor who moved to New York in the 1920s and has the distinction of being the first Somali immigrant to America."[12] After World War II, the United States became interested in Somalia because of its strategic location on the Red Sea, a body of water that sees the circulation of millions of dollars' worth of goods.[13]

Somali Independence 1960-1969

In 1943, the Somali Youth Club, which later became the Somali Youth League, was founded by young urban middle-class Somalis who began to agitate for independence.[14] The Somali Youth League spent years petitioning the United Nations for Somali independence. Rather than granting Somalia independence, the United Nations in 1950 opted to give Italy control over the Somali territories.[15] Historian and Somali studies scholar Safia Aidid shows that, in 1950, "eager to welcome Italy back into the Western camp, Britain, France, and the United States voted on November 21, 1949, for a UN trusteeship under Italian administration."[16] The American vote highlights the role the US played in blocking Somali independence. Italy was granted trusteeship status over Somalia due to the colonial belief that the Somali people were inadequately prepared for independence.[17]

This paternalism is a significant feature of colonialism because Somali people were viewed as children by the European powers. In Abdi Samatar's *Africa's First Democrats*, he recounts the Italian colonial administration's paternalism toward the Somali people. "To add insult to injury," Samatar writes, "the authorities promulgated a new law that stipulated that natives must salute any Italian they came across. The police publicly flogged any Somali who failed to perform such a humiliating act."[18] My own grandfather worked as a busboy for the Italians and had to show deference in the presence of Italians by taking off his hat and bowing. Achille Mbembe also argues that "paternalism had no compunction about expressing itself behind the ideological mask of benevolence and the tawdry cloak of humanism."[19] This same paternalistic ideology shapes the contemporary developmental and humanitarian efforts that represent Somali people as incapable of self-government and thus in need of guidance from the "benevolent" Western powers.

The United Nations institutionalized Italy's relationship to Somalia by creating a ten-year Italian trusteeship with the stipulation that Italy would guide Somalia to independence. The document that marked the legal formalization of the trusteeship is titled "Trusteeship Agreement for the Territory of Somaliland under Italian Administration, adopted by the Trusteeship Council January 27, 1950." Article 3 of the trusteeship agreement described the duties of Italy regarding the nascent Somali territories as follows: "[To] promote the economic advancement and self-sufficiency of the inhabitants, and to this end shall regulate the use of natural resources; encourage the development of fisheries, agriculture, trade and industries; protect the inhabitants against the loss of their lands and resources; and improve the means of transportation and communication."[20]

I shared this archival document with a Somali elder named Ali who had lived through the Italian trusteeship period in Somalia during the 1950s. Ali spoke back to the colonial archives that often erase Somali voices and claimed that he remembers that Italian colonial administrators believed that Somalis were incapable of achieving self-sufficiency. Ali was incensed when he stated, "How could the colonial administrators say we needed to be helped to be self-sufficient, Somalis were self-sufficient long before colonial powers came to Somalia." Ali went on to explain that "the Italians tried to humiliate and control the Somali people, but we fought them at every turn."[21] This spirit of Somali resistance mobilized

Somalis throughout the period of Italian trusteeship. Yet Somali resistance to colonial imposition is not new, as E. R. Turton, a historian of Somalia, shows. "Resistance to the imposition of colonial rule is exemplified by the Herti uprising of 1893, the Ogaden revolts of 1898 and 1901, Marehan resistance in 1913 and an Aulihan rebellion in 1916."[22]

In the spirit of this resistance, the Somali Youth League mobilized the Somali people to challenge this Italian trusteeship. According to Abdi Ismail Samatar and Ahmed I. Samatar, "At this time, the SYL's popularity was growing, almost in proportion to the degree of its suppression by the Italian administration. However, the new Governor, Anzilotti, calculated that the Italians' tenure as trustees of Somalia could be extended to a couple more decades if enough local public opinion was mobilized."[23] The Somali Youth League formulated a vision of a unified Somalia that was free from colonial occupation. Abdinasir Ali, a Somali refugee residing in San Diego, remembers the Somali Youth League: "I remember how excited people in Mogadishu were for the Somali Youth League, we believed that unification was possible." As Abdinasir states, the league desired nothing less than the unification into one republic of the five territories where Somalis make up the majority of the local population: British Somaliland, Italian Somaliland, French Somaliland (Djibouti), the Ogaden in Ethiopia, and the Northern Frontier District in Kenya.[24] Ahmed Kusow, another Somali refugee elder, also remembers this moment in 1959: "On the eve of Somali independence there was so much excitement, Somali people would never tolerate colonialization again, and many of us believed that all the Somali people living in Kenya and Ethiopia would be unified."[25]

The five-pointed star that the Somali Youth League chose as the Somali flag symbolized this platform of uniting the five territories. Ultimately, the league was unable to achieve its goal of uniting the five territories, but that outcome was the result of complex factors, including Ethiopia's resistance to acceding the Ogaden; Kenya's desire to maintain control over the Northern Frontier District; and French Somaliland becoming Djibouti.[26] Another obstacle to unification was Britain's decision to grant the Ogaden to Ethiopia in 1948 and the Northern Frontier District to Kenya in 1960.[27] These actions taken by the British colonial government created decades-long border disputes between Somalia, Kenya, and Ethiopia. Yet, in the months following Somali independence, the Somali Youth League believed unification was an achievable goal. The Republic of Somalia came into being in July 1960, when British and Italian Somaliland merged into one territory. In July 1960, Abdirazak H. Hussein, the president of the Somali Youth League, was elected as the first prime minister of Somalia. Aisha, a Somali refugee living in San Diego, was a little girl when Hussein was elected but vividly remembers his election: "I remember my parents were so excited for the first Somali president; they said Somalia was one of the few African nations to democratically elect its president."[28] Yet this excitement would be short-lived because in less than a decade a brutal dictator would come to power in Somalia.

In the 1970s, the US government also became involved with Somalia as part of a Cold War strategy to spread its influence and deter the rise of communism in Somalia. A speech from Ronald Reagan highlights this stance: "If the Soviets are successful—and it looks more and more as if they will be—then the entire Horn of Africa will be under their influence, if not their control."[29] The US provided military aid to Mohamed Siad Barre in Somalia, revealing America's Cold War tactic of supporting dictatorial regimes.[30]

America's relationship to Siad Barre culminated in Barre meeting with Reagan in the Oval Office.[31]

Cold War/Hot War and the US-Supported Dictatorship of Siad Barre, 1969–1990

In 1969, Siad Barre, at the time a high-ranking general, led a coup d'état to take control of the Somali government. In the 1950s, Barre was a young police officer in the Somali colonial police. By 1969, he had worked his way up to become the highest-ranking general in Somalia. He had also spent time training and learning military tactics in Russia, where he also discovered scientific socialism.[32]

During his rise to power, Barre set out to establish scientific socialism as the official doctrine of the Somali state.[33] Aisha, a grandmother and Somali refugee living in San Diego, relates her memories of Barre's rise to power: "Barre's coup happened so suddenly and without much violence; once in power, he set out to establish scientific socialism, but we all knew that was just a guise to hide his corruption."[34] Aisha's comments underscore how scientific socialism was the Somali government's policy in name only because in practice the dictatorship operated under a system of nepotism. Barre's friends and members of his family, regardless of their lack of qualifications, were appointed to the highest positions of the dictatorship.[35]

By giving preferential treatment to members of his clan, a political instrument readily available to him, Barre alienated other clans. He mobilized the Somali clan system to concentrate power in his administration, a move that recalls the British colonial administration's deployment of customary laws that gave centralized power to clan leadership.[36] As a result, the clan became a critical political tool for those seeking to consolidate power in Somalia.

Barre's rise to power was as much conditioned by the legacy of British colonialism as it was by the power vacuum created by Cold War politics. According to Mohamed Haji Ingiriis, who draws on the work of Alice Bettis Hashim, "General Siad Barre ruled Somalia with an iron fist for most of his regime (1969-91). Hashim, in her evaluation of Somalia under his regime, shows that the regime was based on 'a monolithic totalitarian structure.' Its dominant philosophy was to master the technology of power so as to master destiny."[37] Barre allocated prominent positions and resources to his tribe, the Marehan clan. The Barre-led administration gave preferential treatment to them in private industry and public office: the most desirable business contracts, jobs, and land were reserved for members of the Marehan clan.[38] I conducted a series of oral histories with Somali elders living in City Heights, San Diego, regarding the Somali dictatorship. Some of the elders I spoke to had strong feelings regarding the Barre dictatorship and the favoritism shown to the Marehan clan. During one of these sessions, a well-respected elder in the community shared his recollections of life under Barre's dictatorship. The elder, who went by the name Osman Hussein, referred to the dictator as "Afwayne," which loosely translates to "big mouth":

> Afwayne only helped people who were Marehan; people like me who are Hawiye—we could not find any jobs because all the good jobs went to Afwayne's relatives. I was very angry because even if you were educated or hard-working, you could not get a good paying job if you were not Marehan. We couldn't even complain about this because if people caught you complaining about Afwayne, you would end up in jail.[39]

Osman's use of the term "Afwayne" to denigrate the dictator is one manifestation of infrapolitics: the tools used by those with limited resources to resist state power.[40] Osman belongs to a minority clan and utilized infrapolitics because the dictator was known to be violent toward his detractors. The dictator deployed his executive powers to execute and jail anyone who dared to question his rule.[41] Barre's preferential treatment toward the Marehan clan fueled animosity between the Marehan and other clans.

Despite the atrocities' committed by Barre, the United States supported Barre's regime by outfitting him with weapons and providing financial assistance.[42] According to Peter J. Schraeder, a scholar on US foreign policy, the United States provided more than $800 million to the Barre regime.[43] Catherine Besteman estimates the figure at closer to a billion: "During the 1980s, the United States made Somalia its second-largest recipient of foreign aid in Africa, granting Barre hundreds upon hundreds of millions of dollars in military and economic aid. Analysts estimate that Barre received over a billion dollars in foreign aid from international sources during the 1980s, an astounding figure for a lightly populated, arid country with few natural resources."[44]

The US government fostered a relationship with Barre to wrest control of East Africa from the Soviet Union and thereby access the lucrative trade and military routes on the Horn of Africa that connected India, the Middle East, and Africa.[45] The United States supported Barre during the 1978 Ogaden War with Ethiopia as a way to cement this relationship. During a 1980 presidential debate with Reagan, Jimmy Carter stated: "Our agreement with Somalia is a limited one. It is one of three we recently signed in the region. The other two were with Oman and Kenya. Each of these agreements will help us maintain a better military balance in that part of the world and therefore to protect our security interests and those of the states of the region."[46] The Carter administration also provided military support to Barre to secure US imperial interests in Somalia. Donna Jackson, a public policy scholar, explains that "the United States had provided aid to the tune of some $80 million to Somalia from 1954 to 1970."[47] In addition to money, the United States also supplied weapons to Somalia in the war effort, while the Soviet Union furnished weapons to Ethiopia.[48]

In fact, the United States had been influential in convincing Britain to grant the Ogaden—a region in western Ethiopia with a large Somali population—to Ethiopia.[49] It is precisely due to this border dispute that a full-scale war broke out between Somalia and Ethiopia in 1977. Barre went to war with Ethiopia over the disputed Ogaden region, and the fighting culminated in an Ethiopian victory. Somalia's defeat in the war solidified Ethiopia's claim to the region. Russia provided aerial support to the Ethiopian army, which helped Ethiopia gain a strategic advantage.[50] Russian fighter planes dropped bombs on Somali troops, resulting in significant Somali casualties and a Somali surrender.[51] Ali Hussein, a young soldier during the Ogaden War, now resides in San Diego. He remembers US involvement in the war: "During the war, Russia was supporting Ethiopia and the US backed Somalia, yet many of the Somali soldiers were resentful of American involvement even though we needed their resources."[52] Ali's statement underscores that Somalis were not passive to American Cold War strategies but rather resented foreign intrusion into Somali politics. With the displacement of thousands of Somalis, the Ogaden War produced the first Somali refugee crisis. The United States continued to fund the Barre government despite his well-documented history of human right abuses.

The *Chicago Tribune* quoted Rep. Howard Wole of Michigan as admitting partial US culpability for what he described as "the tragedy that is evolving in front of our eyes right now... because it was the United States that had propped up the incredibly repressive, corrupt regime of Siad Barre."[53] Besteman also makes clear how US support for the Barre regime waned only with end of the Cold War: "The regime's heinous actions became important to US politicians only after communism collapsed and it was difficult to justify US support for such a dictator any longer."[54] The US government's support for Barre did not align with the country's public image as a defender of human rights, yet, indeed, the United States does support dictators and has a well-established track record of committing human rights abuses. Amina Hassan, a Somali nurse in San Diego, argues that "Barre was a violent and cruel dictator that the US government continued to support. He had jailed many people simply for opposing his policies."[55] A 1989 Amnesty International report buttresses many of Amina's claims regarding Barre, stating, "Extrajudicial executions of suspected government opponents and [the Somali Nationalist Movement] supporters were widespread and thousands of civilians fleeing Hargeisa were deliberately killed by government artillery bombardment."[56] Abdi Hassan, a Somali poet who lived in Mogadishu during the 1970s, says, "The Americans were responsible for supporting the Barre regime but refused to acknowledge their role in the collapse of the Somali state. We need to see the long history of US imperialism in Somalia."[57] Hassan's recollection of the Barre regime and American involvement underscores how the historical amnesia practiced by the United States with regard to Somalia is countered by a Somali refugee epistemology that offers an alternative historical record of America's relationship to Somalia.

Like Hassan, Mary Dudziak argues that the battleground of the Cold War was located in third world countries like Somalia.[58] For many third world countries, the Cold War was a "hot war." Yet rather than being a passive pawn of the United States, Barre manipulated Cold War politics to his benefit, repeatedly shifting his allegiance between the United States and the Soviet Union as if playing a dangerous game of hot potato. Initially this strategy worked in Barre's favor because he received military funding from both superpowers. His regime imported arms amounting to $750 million between 1976 and 1980.[59]

The financial and political support the United States and Russia provided to the dictator helped him maintain his grip over Somalia. Lidwien Kapteijns suggests that US military aid to Barre's regime from 1980–88 amounted to $163.5 million.[60] In August 1980, the United States and Somalia "signed a ten-year base rights access to the joint port-airfield facilities at Barbera and Mogadishu."[61] The United States was particularly interested in establishing miliary bases on the coast of Somalia as a way to project power and deploy its naval and air forces across the Indian Ocean and to the Middle East. It is for this reason that the United States continued to support the Barre regime financially and politically.

The Siad Barre dictatorship lasted twenty-one years: from 1969, when he initiated a coup d'état to take control of the Somali government, to the 1991 collapse of the Somali state. During this time, Barre galvanized his power and monopolized the means of violence, all with the military support of the United States.[62] Asha Ahmed, a Somali refugee in San Diego, remembers the 1970s "as a turbulent time for Somalis. From colonialism to a dictatorship, Somalis kept trading one form of unfreedom for another. Yet we did not lose hope; there were many Somali people that resisted the

Barre regime."[63] Asha's testimony is particularly telling because it reveals the ways in which Somalis traded one form of unfreedom under Italian trusteeship for another: a brutal dictatorship. Yet Asha's recollection of the Barre regime ended with resistance, highlighting Somali people's long legacy of resistance to colonialism, dictatorship, and, eventually, US imperialism. In 1993, Somali resistance would directly clash with the US military in what the latter dubbed "Operation Restore Hope."

Transnational War in Somalia: 1991 to Present

The so-called Somali civil war is often narrated in the news media as a primordial tribal animosity that turned deadly.[64] This framework ignores how the millions of dollars' of arms that flooded Somalia from the Soviet Union and the United States in the 1970s and 1980s enabled and intensified the devastation caused by the Somali civil war. The Somali civil war began in 1991, when forces from the United Somali Congress ousted Siad Barre from power. An article from Minnesota Public Radio is typical of the way US media coverage highlights the discourse of tribalism associated with the Somali civil war: "Following the collapse of the dictatorship that ruled Somalia in the early 1990s, a renewed focus on tribalism fueled civil war, forcing hundreds of thousands to flee their homes."[65] To disrupt this narrative, I argue that the Somali civil war was not a tribal war but a transnational war involving the United States, Italy, and Great Britain.[66] According to Faysal Ahmed, a San Diego community organizer and survivor of the Somali civil war, "The newspapers lied about the Somali civil war: they believe the war is a clan war but ignore the fact that the armies of ten different countries were in Somalia in 1993 during the Somali civil war. The news media would have you believe that Somalis are primitive Africans that love war. The truth is no country loves war more than the US."[67] In his analysis, Faysal shifts the focus from the correlation of Somalia and Somali people with violence and tribalism by exposing the violence of US militarism. Faysal's critique of US imperialism is in conversation with the work of scholar David Vine, who argues that the United States does not go to war—rather, the United States *is* war. Vine's *The United States of War* shows that the United States has been at war every year since its founding.[68] In 1993, Somalia became the new site of American warfare.

In 1991, the war escalated when Mohamed Farah Aidid, of the United Somali Congress, and his forces reached the capital city of Mogadishu with the aim of ousting Barre, resulting in Barre fleeing the capital. The confrontation between these two military forces produced havoc in the capital and created a mass refugee exodus into neighboring Kenya. Ahmed Ali, a Somali refugee residing in San Diego, remembers this moment: "None of us imagined that Barre would fall or that the war would last for as long as it did; it was for this reason that very few people fled Mogadishu initially."[69] Despite the unfathomability of the collapse of the Barre regime, Aidid's military force pressured the dictator to retreat into neighboring Kenya. The ousting of the dictator in 1991 produced a power vacuum in Somalia because Barre had centralized state power around himself. Following this power vacuum, the Somali Nationalist Movement, led by Ali Mahdi, emerged, claiming to be the rightful successors to the Somali state.[70] The leading Somali military factions were the Somali Nationalist Movement and the United Somali Congress. These disparate militias battled for control of the capital and claimed to represent the interests of the Somali people. The armed conflict between these factions produced turmoil that lasted decades. The rival factions at the time were divided along clan lines, with Mohamed Farah Aidid rallying the Hawiye clan and Ali Mahdi of the Somali Nationalist Movement mobilizing the Isaq clan. Ali Hussein owned a small clothing shop in Mogadishu during the war and remembers the ousting of Barre: "Senseless violence was happening all over Mogadishu after the fall of Barre. Members of the Hawiye and Marehan clans fought for control over the government, and innocent people were caught in the cross fire."[71] A World Bank report offers a similar appraisal of the events following Barre's defeat: "The ouster of the Barre regime was followed not by a replacement government but by a prolonged period of violent anarchy and warfare. Armed conflict raged across southern Somalia through 1991 and 1992."[72]

In 1992, the United Nations sprang into action to address the humanitarian crises produced by the Somali civil war. The secretary-general of the United Nations, Boutros Boutros-Ghali declared:

> The involvement of the United Nations in search for peace in Somalia began with an attempt, as I took office in January 1992, to bring about a negotiated ceasefire in Mogadishu. . . . As the famine toll rose, reaching appalling proportions in mid-1992, it became clear that a much larger force was needed to protect relief supplies and that it had to be deployed quickly, whether or not the faction leaders agreed.[73]

Boutros-Ghali's claim that "it became clear that a much larger force was needed" signals the rise of militarized humanitarianism, which Neda Atanasoski explains as the shift from the Cold War as a legitimizing apparatus for US military interventions in Africa to the emergence of humanitarianism as a legitimizing apparatus in the 1990s.[74] Boutros-Ghali's plea for militarized humanitarianism foreshadowed the series of events that led to the escalation of military violence in Somalia. According to a historian who was on the ground with US military forces in Somalia, "A multinational force led by the United States was allowed to use all necessary force to accomplish its humanitarian mission. It was the first time in history the United Nations had elected to intervene in the internal affairs of a country without having received a request to do so from the country's government."[75]

The circulation of images of starving children in the news media inspired the United Nations to take action in Somalia. Political theorist Bernard Cohen writes, "By focusing daily on the starving children in Somalia, a pictorial story tailor-made for television, TV mobilized the conscience of the nation's public institutions, compelling the government into a policy of intervention for humanitarian reasons."[76] These images relied on the discourse of African suffering to legitimize US militarism. This discourse posits that suffering is a natural feature of African life, one that can only be interrupted by Western intervention.[77] According to a BBC news article from 1992: "US troops have arrived in Somalia in a bid to aid thousands of starving locals. The American marines landed just before dawn. Their mission is to spearhead the arrival of 35,000 troops from a dozen countries assembled as part of a US-led multinational operation to crack down on looting and extortion that has prevented food getting through."[78]

In 1992, the United Nations deployed a multinational military force, led by the United States, to Somalia as a response to the situation. According to embedded historian Dennis Mroczkowski, "Allowing the United States to lead the force satisfied one of the few demands placed by President Bush upon the offer of troops."[79] Other countries that contributed forces included: Australia, Bangladesh, Belgium, Botswana, Canada, Egypt, Ethiopia, France, Germany, Greece, India, Ireland, Italy, Kuwait, Morocco, New Zealand, Nigeria, Norway, Pakistan, Saudi Arabia, Spain, Sweden, Tunisia, Turkey, United Arab Emirates, the United Kingdom, and Zimbabwe.[80] The large number of countries involved reveals that the Somali civil war was as much a global phenomenon as it was an internal national conflict.

Considering US leadership of this taskforce, I posit that US militarism played an important role in the Somali civil war and the subsequent flight of millions of Somali refugees from their homeland. Amina Sheik, a Somali refugee nurse in San Diego, is critical of America's role in the Somali civil war: "American forces contributed to the Somali civil war, burned down villages, and made the situation worse in Somalia, but once American soldiers left Somalia, the US pretends that they have not been involved in Somalia or are responsible for Somali refugees."[81] Amina's analysis shows that the US military withdrew from Somalia in 1994, leaving the landscape and its people in tatters. The devastation created by the Somali civil war is not limited to the loss of life but also entails the destruction of critical infrastructure.

Following the devastation and loss of life caused by the Somali civil war, the UN secretary-general mobilized UN security forces to Somalia; initially numbering fifty soldiers, the security forces were deployed to protect aid workers. The presence of UN security forces increased in a matter of months. The logic behind troop deployment to Somalia is underscored by UN Resolution 751: "On the very day of his arrival my special representative was informed by Mr. Ali Mahdi, that the latter's faction of the United Somali Congress accepted by the deployment of up to fifty United Nations military observers to monitor the ceasefire in Mogadishu and agreed that these observers would be in uniform and unarmed."[82] The resolution spotlights the shift from humanitarianism to peacekeeping as the organizing structure for military presence in Somalia. The fifty UN soldiers, who had originally been sent to ensure the protection of aid workers, were utilized to enforce a ceasefire agreement. Ali Mahdi was asked by the United Nations to sanction troop deployment to Somalia because he claimed to be the sole sovereign power in Somalia.[83] The United Nations requested Ali's approval to mask the fact that they were committing an aggressive military action against a sovereign nation.

In 1993, the United Nations placed an embargo on the importation of weapons into Somalia.[84] The US government's support for this embargo underscores the country's historical amnesia: the United States had supplied many of the weapons that caused untold destruction in Somalia during the civil war. Terry Atlas explains that "in one of the most extraordinary flip-flops in the US-Soviet rivalry, the Carter and Reagan administrations poured economic and military aid into Somalia in return for influence and access to the Soviet-built naval and air base at Berbera on the Indian Ocean coast."[85] I juxtapose this quote with the historical memory of a Somali refugee living in San Diego named Hamdi Nur, who says he "directly witnessed the shipment of weapons and arms that the US was sending to Barre, so I find it laughable when American movies like *Black Hawk Down* claim Americans only came to Somalia for humanitarian reasons and aren't partly responsible for the destruction those weapons created."[86]

Therefore, the US media's depiction of the Somali civil war as indigenous tribal warfare is contested by Somali peoples' living memories of the war. Somali oral histories provide an alternative epistemology to both state-mediated archives and narratives produced by the US media as well as images of Somali "savagery" depicted in popular films like *Black Hawk Down*.

Following the UN embargo, the United Somali Congress and the Somali Nationalist Movement planned a ceasefire with the goal of negotiating an end to the war. The arrival of American troops in Somalia disrupted the ceasefire and escalated the war. UN Resolution 767 best encapsulates the acceleration of military forces in Somalia. This UN resolution proposed the deployment of four additional security units to Somalia. The presence of UN troops represented more than a deployment of security personnel; such a large force had the characteristics of an invading army. In a letter dated November 24, 1992, the UN secretary-general noted, "Another disturbing trend, which has evolved in recent weeks, apparently at the instigation of local faction leaders, is the widespread perception among Somalis that the United Nations has decided to abandon its policy of cooperation and is planning to 'invade' the country."[87] The United Nations refused to acknowledge that its military force functioned like an invading army, choosing to ignore the sovereignty of Somalia.

On the surface, the UN military operation in Somalia appeared to be humanitarian in nature, but it functioned like a military invasion. The testimony of Asho Noor, who grew up in Mogadishu in the 1980s, illuminates Somali views of US intervention in Somalia: "'Operation Restore Hope' was a US military invasion that did nothing to help the situation. The US was mostly interested in securing access to the Somali coast and establishing US military bases."[88] Moreover, this operation was the first time in UN history that military force was utilized as part of a humanitarian campaign. UN Secretary-General Boutros-Ghali explained this historical precedent:

> The resulting operation, which was to be known as the United Task Force (UNITAF) and code-named "Operation Restore Hope" by the United States, set a new historical precedent for the United Nations.... The United Nations for the first time in its history authorized a group of member states to use military force not under United Nations command for humanitarian ends in an internal conflict, albeit one with serious ramification for regional peace and security because of the huge influx of Somali refugees, many of them armed, into neighboring countries.[89]

The principle of "deterrence of aggression against sovereign states" did not apply to Somalia; rather, Somalia was represented as a space imbued with so much irrational violence that similar force was needed to subdue it. The United Nations was more concerned about armed refugees entering neighboring nations than about armed and violent coalition forces entering Somalia. I interviewed Somali refugees about their encounters with the UN taskforce, and Faysal Ahmed disputed the United Nations' version of events: "Very few people in Mogadishu at the time believed that the task force was in Somalia for humanitarian reasons. We saw the UN soldiers and American soldiers as an invading army."[90] Juxtaposing Faysal's testimony with the UN secretary-general's statement reveals the ways in which violence is projected onto the Somali people and spatially identified with the country of Somalia to disguise the violence of imperialism.

Conclusion

In 1994, the US military withdrew from Somalia after Operation Restore Hope failed spectacularly and publicly with the deaths of eighteen Marines. Yet by 1991, six hundred thousand Somalis had been displaced as a result of the war.[91] Operation Restore Hope would be remembered and memorialized in the film *Black Hawk Down* as a conflict between Somali "savagery" and American heroism.[92] This film was devoid of any historical or political nuance and erased the role of US imperialism in destabilizing the Somali state.[93] American soldiers were simply innocent victims unfairly and irrationally assaulted by Somalis who should have been grateful for US intervention. As Ayaan Jamac, a young Somali activist in San Diego, claims, "In *Black Hawk Down*, Somalis are the bad guys and American soldiers are the good guys who have to kill the bad guys because they have no choice."[94]

In this chapter, I traced the colonial and imperial histories that produced the conditions of possibility for the Somali civil war. The Somali refugee crisis is also situated within a global refugee crisis that includes over 79 million refugees worldwide.[95] This refugee crisis is made possible by the heightened militarism that marked the twentieth century. There was a mass exodus of Somali refugees into Western countries, such as the United States, Canada, and Great Britain, following the withdrawal of US forces. In 1994, the United States began accepting Somali refugees in large numbers.[96] As this chapter demonstrates, the US military crossed the borders of Somalia long before Somali refugees crossed the borders of the United States. In September 1992, US Marines from Camp Pendleton, San Diego, were deployed to Somalia, and in October of that same year, the first wave of Somali refugees arrived in San Diego; hence, US militarism produces refugees.

A *San Diego Union-Tribune* article from 1992 details experiences of the first group of Somali refugees to come to San Diego:

> The flight is 255, the gate 13. The arrival is 11:08. Abdiweli Heibeh knows them all by heart now, these numbers of hope fulfilled. For weeks he's been coming to Lindbergh Field to meet that plane at that gate at that time, to greet still more relatives fleeing the twin tragedies of civil war and famine in Somalia. So now he knows another number, 54, the total of his family members who call San Diego home. "This is a safe haven," he says.[97]

This exodus of Somali refugees is conditioned by a long history of British colonialism, Italian trusteeship, and US imperialism. Faduma was one of the first Somali refugees to arrive in San Diego in 1992, and she remembers this moment as one of "sadness—that is what we felt when we arrived in San Diego. No one wants to leave their home behind."[98] The first Somali refugees who arrived at San Diego brought with them more than just a history of colonial and imperial violence: they also brought a long history of poetry, storytelling, and political resistance to authoritarianism in its many manifestations. US imperialism followed British and Italian colonialism in creating the conditions of possibility for the Somali civil war and the subsequent flight of millions of Somalis from their homeland. The canonical portrayal of the Somali civil war as simply a matter of tribal warfare, and the media depiction of US military intervention in Somalia as a humanitarian operation, fails to account for the historical and enduring impact of US militarism on

Somali refugee life. The United States has remained interested in Somalia because "Somalia's northern coast borders the Gulf of Aden, which leads to Bab el-Mandeb, a narrow chokepoint through which all maritime traffic from the Mediterranean Sea to the Indian Ocean must pass."[99] It is for this reason that Somalia continues to be a target of US militarism.

In the popular media, Somalia has become synonymous with anarchy, piracy, and terrorism thanks to films such as *Black Hawk Down* and *Captain Phillips*, which portray Somalis as violent savages hungry for war. Yet for much of Somalia's history it was known as a nation of poets.[100] Somali poetry has historically been political, with Somali poets providing some of the most eloquent critiques of colonialism, imperialism, and nepotism. As Somali studies scholar Safia Aidid explains, "A predominantly oral culture, poetic traditions continue to maintain an important social function in the daily lives of Somalis, often employed as a pedagogical tool for communication, consciousness-raising, and preserving history."[101] Contemporary Somali poets such as Warsan Shire have gained international attention and have worked to alter the dominant narratives of Somalis as warlords, pirates, and terrorists.

Although the United States continues to deny the role it played in the Somali civil war, Somali refugees can never escape the collective trauma that continues to shape their lived experiences. My lived experience reflects this, as the specters of war continue to haunt my family, producing a collective trauma that might take generations to heal. Mirroring my family's journey, the collapse of the Somali state forced thousands of Somali refugees into neighboring Kenya. In the next chapter, I will examine Somali refugees' experiences in the Dadaab refugee camp in Kenya. Having fled militarized violence in Somalia, Somalis were then greeted by a carceral refugee camp. Many of the Somali refugees who arrived in San Diego had spent many years in the Dadaab refugee camp. To this day, Kenya is still home to the largest Somali refugee population.[102]

2 *The Carceral Refugee Camp*

Abdi Hamza is a Somali refugee who volunteers his time mentoring Somali refugee youths. He first came to San Diego in 1996 after spending four years in the Dadaab refugee camp. Abdi recollects his experiences in the Dadaab refugee camp:

> You have to remember our lives didn't start in San Diego, and they don't end in San Diego; we still have family in the Dadaab refugee camps. Many of us spend our whole lives in those camps, and some of us never leave. The camps aren't a temporary place until we get resettled; they are our homes. We learn how to survive and how to build community in the camps, and we bring that knowledge to San Diego. I am from the camps as much as I am from Somalia.[1]

A temporary space like the refugee camp can grant a sense of permanency to refugees. After fleeing their homes in Somalia, refugees built new homes in the Dadaab refugee camp. For many refugees, home is not a fixed location but a space sustained by familial and community relations. Few Somalis relocated to the United States directly from Somalia; rather, most spent years in a second city of resettlement before reaching US shores. The Dadaab refugee camp in Kenya is one such waystation, and it houses the largest Somali refugee population in the world.[2] The premier destination for Somali refugees fleeing the civil war, Dadaab became a place where Somali refugees created survival strategies to navigate their new, if somewhat impermanent, lives.

What did Somali refugees encounter in the Dadaab refugee camp when they fled the violence of war? What do we learn about the Dadaab refugee camp if we privilege Somali refugees' lived experiences in the camp? The dominant narrative is that the Dadaab refugee camp is a space of humanitarian benevolence and rescue. As the UN high commissioner for refugees, Filippo Grandi, stated in a 2017 visit to Dadaab, "We need to extend protection to them [Somali refugees] when they are in host countries and to help them return home when they choose to do so."[3] Yet a former resident of Dadaab whom I interviewed, Hussein Ali, counters Grandi's idea of "protection," arguing that "camp officials don't care about Somali refugees; we are treated like prisoners in there with no freedom of movement."[4] To echo Ali's refugee epistemology, I argue that the Dadaab refugee camp is not a site of humanitarian benevolence but rather of humanitarian violence. The Dadaab refugee camp is a carceral space where Somali refugees' movements and bodies are policed. Somali refugees' lived experiences highlight the intersection between militarism and policing. Somali refugees fled the violence of militarized humanitarianism in 1993 only to then encounter humanitarian violence in the refugee camp in the form of policing and surveillance. To reveal the ways in which the Dadaab refugee camp functions as a carceral space, I treat Somali stories as a refugee analytic that shows that the refugee camp and Somalia are not discrete spaces: they are interconnected spaces where violence, family, politics, and memories coalesce.

By employing a carceral studies framework alongside a critical refugee studies analytic, I interweave Somali refugees' experiences with police violence in the refugee camps and their encounters with ongoing forms of police violence in San Diego. These two sites function as spaces of confinement for Somali refugees. Moreover, in this chapter I look at the world from the perspective of refugees and argue that by centering our analysis on refugee experiences, we can learn the complex and myriad ways that state violence functions and the creative strategies refugees employ to resist this violence. Moreover, I relate my own experiences living in the Dadaab refugee camp from 1991 to 1996 as part of a Somali refugee epistemology.

Dadaab Kenya: Policing the Refugee Camp

In 1991, throngs of displaced Somali refugees fled to neighboring Kenya at the height of the Somali civil war. The Dadaab refugee camp was constructed as a temporary site to house these fleeing refugees. Although Dadaab was initially built to provide sanctuary for ninety thousand refugees, in a matter of years that number grew to three hundred thousand refugees, wildly exceeding the capacity of the refugee camp.[5] A significant portion of refugees in Dadaab spend on average five to ten years awaiting resettlement. Somali refugees have stayed in Dadaab for long stretches of time because of the protracted nature of the resettlement process. Globally, refugees are in a protracted situation, with an average stay in the refugee camp equaling twenty-six years.[6] Therefore, refugee camps can effectively become semipermanent homes for refugees. The Kenyan state decided to place the refugee camp in Dadaab because it cost the state very little: Dadaab is in one of the most arid and unlivable parts of Kenya. According to Marc-Antoine Perouse de Montclos and Peter Kagwanja, a scholar at the Center for Refugee Studies, "This was accompanied by a shift in government policy in favor of confining asylum seekers to camps located in the semi-arid areas of Northern Kenya, away from the main economic activities and urban centers."[7] The land in Dadaab is not conducive to growing crops, and the region is known to be lawless. New arrivals had little choice but to build a home in such a dangerous and undesirable location. The placement of Somali refugees in Dadaab is an indictment of the Kenyan state's disregard for the lives of Somali refugees.

Moreover, the Kenyan state's policy toward Somali refugees is shaped by decades of political strife between Kenya and Somalia.[8] This tension can be traced to Britain granting the Northern Frontier District to Kenya in 1960.[9] This region of Kenya is populated by a large ethnic Somali population. The Somali state claimed that the Northern Frontier District should become a part of Somalia. Therefore, Somalis living in the northern region of Kenya have faced decades of persecution and unfair harassment by the Kenyan state, which views them as a security threat. Abdi Nur is a Somali refugee who spent a decade in Kenya, and he believes that "Somalis are treated like terrorists in Kenya. We are all assumed to be criminal; that's why there is so much police harassment of Somalis."[10] A 2013 Human Rights Watch report, *"You Are All Terrorists": Kenyan Police Abuse of Refugees in Nairobi*, supports Nur's critique of the Kenyan state and the criminalization of Somali refugees. According to this report, "Absent effective Kenyan accountability mechanisms to prevent police abuses and to punish Kenyan police officers who perpetrate human rights abuses against refugees," Somali refugees have had to create their own strategies to navigate Kenyan police.[11]

The largest Somali community in Kenya outside of Dadaab is in Eastleigh, a large, segregated neighborhood. In this neighborhood, Somalis are not only segregated from Kenyan society but also experience racial profiling and police raids. Although the Somalis who live outside the refugee camp have more mobility, they are still not free from state surveillance and they experience limited options for mobility due to the discrimination they experience. In addition to the security apparatus aimed at Somali refugees in Kenya, the United Nations High Commissioner for Refugees (UNHCR) runs the camp as a site of containment rather than a space of rescue. In 1990, the UNHCR took control of the Dadaab refugee camp. The Dadaab refugee camp is run by UNHCR staff and volunteers. According to Catherine Besteman, "The UNHCR holds sole authority for recognizing and registering refugees." She adds that "detailed, on-the-ground ethnographic studies of the Dadaab camps provide ample evidence of these claims, documenting the ways in which camp policies and practices disempower refugees, who are often treated with contempt and condescension and denied any voice in democratic decision-making processes."[12] Therefore, the refugee camp is a site of containment for stateless people who fled their host country and are denied opportunities to resettle elsewhere. Aisha Hassan, a Somali refugee who spent four years in Dadaab between 1996–2000, says, "The UNHCR doesn't care about Somali refugees, I never once felt that they were there to help us, I felt like the camp was a detention center." In the eyes of Somali refugees, the Dadaab refugee camp functions like a detention center where freedom of movement is restricted by both the UNHCR and the Kenyan state.

The 2006 Refugees Act in Kenyan law highlights the constraints imposed on refugee mobility: "Every refugee and asylum seeker shall—(a) be issued with a refugee identity card or pass in the prescribed form; and (b) be permitted to remain in Kenya in accordance with the provisions of this Act."[13] This law stipulates that refugees must secure formal approval from UNHCR officials to leave the camps. I remember how, when my family lived in Dadaab, my mother was forbidden from finding work outside the camp and was solely reliant on refugee food rations to take care of us. My mother was frustrated by the limitations placed on refugee mobility, stating, "How did they expect me to raise four kids with these food rations and they won't let me leave the refugee camp to find work?"[14]

The 2016 revised Refugees Act further restricts refugee mobility, as refugees cannot "leave the designated refugee camp without the permission of the Refugee Camp Officer."[15] Therefore refugee camp officers have significant power over refugees. Article 13 of the Universal Declaration of Human Rights considers freedom of movement a human right.[16] As a consequence, the Kenyan state infringes on the basic human rights of Somali refugees. Ladan Diriye related during an interview, "Somali refugees are human, too. We should not be forced to live in squalor in a refugee camp and have our movements restricted. Why should we ask permission in order to leave the camps? If we have to ask permission to leave, how are we any different from prisoners?"[17] Ladan's story provides a refugee analytic that equates the camp with prison because Somali refugees must negotiate with a variety of state and nonstate agents to leave. A large percentage of Somali refugees are pastoral nomads who value freedom of movement; yet they are confined in the refugee camp.[18] In 2021, the Kenyan state acknowledged the restrictions placed on refugees under Kenyan law and "that, for a long time, the greatest hindrance to refugee self-reliance has been a hostile legal and policy framework."[19] The curtailment of Somali refugees' mobility extends beyond the camp since many also encounter the surveillance of the Kenyan police once they leave the camps.

Somali refugees routinely experience harassment and abuse from the Kenyan police. Officers customarily demand bribes from Somali refugees, often with little repercussions or direct scrutiny by the state. In an Al Jazeera article documenting one refugee's experience with the Kenyan police, Abdinassir Ismail states, "The policeman alleged my refugee identity card had expired. The truth is that it was still valid. He asked for a bribe. I had 1,000 shillings, equivalent to $12."[20] Abdinassir's experience highlights the police abuse that Somali refugees experience in Kenya. In this story, the police officer repudiated the refugee's claims, which reveals the state's inability to believe refugees. According to Human Rights Watch, as of 2013, the Kenyan government has not "prosecuted anyone responsible for the abuses, fueling the well-documented culture of impunity in Kenya's law enforcement agencies that appears to have encouraged the latest wave of police abuses in Nairobi."[21] There is a lack of accountability within the Kenyan police with regard to their treatment of Somali refugees.

Somali refugees have limited means for legal redress since their complaints regarding police abuse are consistently dismissed by the Kenyan state. Somali refugees are not afforded the same civil liberties as citizens in Kenya; they are not granted the protections that come with citizenship as a legal marker of inclusion. Refugees are by definition people without a state who have been violently expelled from their home countries and legally excluded from access to citizenship in the countries in which they seek refuge. Yet despite the bleakness of this refugee condition, Somali refugees have made homes out of the myriad spaces in which they have found themselves. My mother relied on an intricate network of relatives to help her navigate life in Dadaab. Her sisters helped with babysitting while my mother went to collect resources. My mother and her relatives shared food with each other and helped each other rebuild their tents after they burned down. This network of support is critical in light of the UNHCR staff's apathy toward refugees and the Kenyan police's contempt for Somalis. Hamdi, a Somali who relocated to San Diego from Dadaab in 2012, explains that "many refugees tried to tell UNHCR officials about Kenyan police and how they would rob us of what little money we had, and they did nothing."[22]

In addition to police abuse, the Kenyan state produced a series of policies systemically designed to prevent Somali refugees from integrating into wider Kenyan society. Under the 2021 Refugee Act, a refugee can be fined and imprisoned for "knowingly misleading any refugee officer or authorized officer seeking information material to the exercise of any of her/his powers under this Act."[23] Yet this policy can lead to disproportionate arrests and fines of Somali refugees because, according to Hamdi, "many refugee officers believe that Somali refugees are liars and cannot be trusted, which means a lot of innocent people are fined because of this belief."[24] Hamdi's testimony highlights how Kenyan state agents, including refugee officers and Kenyan police, work together to enforce the criminalization of Somali refugees. An investigative report by Human Rights Watch detailed this abuse: "Human Rights Watch spoke to dozens of Somali refugees who described how police patrolling the border areas near Liboi had stopped their vehicles—carrying an average of around 25 women, children, and men—to extort money from them in exchange for free passage to the camps.

Refugees told Human Rights Watch that police sometimes held young children hostage to force their parents to pay money to secure their release."[25] As this report demonstrates, Somali refugees' experiences with police abuse reveal the carceral nature of the Somali refugee condition in Kenya. In light of these experiences, Somali refugees grew to distrust state agents as a strategy of resistance and survival. Somali refugees regarded Kenyan state agents as people who at best ignored the needs of refugees and at worst regularly exploited refugees for profit. The Kenyan police represent the most visible and violent manifestation of the state's neglect and abuse of Somali refugees. Moreover, the Kenyan government does little to regulate police abuses directed at Somali refugees. Rather than regulate police abuse directed at Somali refugees, the Kenyan state in 2016 made plans to return Somali refugees to Somalia, citing security concerns that refugee camps were hotbeds for terrorism.[26] Therefore, the violence of the Kenyan state is elided by shifting the focus on Somali refugees as sources of violence and threats to Kenya's internal security. In the absence of any intervention from the Kenyan state, Somali refugees developed a repertoire of strategies to circumvent these police abuses.

The Refugee Repertoire

One of these strategies involves sharing information with each other regarding the location of upcoming police raids. By sharing this critical information with a tight-knit circle of other refugees, Somalis created a warning system that helped them avoid police violence. In the face of a Kenyan state that was hostile to their presence, Somali refugees exercised ingenuity; despite the totalitarian nature of the refugee camp, Somali refugees still found ways to have agency in their lives. To spotlight this agency, I offer the stories of Somalis who survived the refugee camps and managed to build new lives in America.

Safia is a longtime resident of City Heights and a fierce advocate for refugees and immigrants. She spent four years in the Dadaab refugee camp in the early 1990s. During one of my interviews with her, Safia explained the tools Somali refugees utilized to circumvent police surveillance in the camp: "All of us worked together to save ourselves from the police; if they came looking for a suspect, we just pretended that we didn't speak Swahili."[27] Thus, Somali refugees produced tools to resist state violence that were not explicitly political; yet, the resistance strategies were political in their disruption of the normal functioning of state power. Safia's decision to feign ignorance of Swahili during her encounter with the Kenyan police is an example of the "refugee repertoire," by which I mean the collection of shared strategies deployed by Somali refugees to resist government oppression and navigate life in the refugee camp. Drawing from a collective well of knowledge, Somalis have had to develop counter-policing strategies due to the routine and unchecked nature of police violence directed at Somali refugees in Kenya.

Policing in the refugee camps is not limited to the actions of the Kenyan police but includes a litany of ways in which Somali refugees' bodies are policed and managed. Humanitarian workers in the Dadaab refugee camp control the food intake of Somali refugees; the policing of refugee bodies underscores the ways the refugee camp functions as a carceral space. In *Humanitarian Violence*, Neda Atanasoski argues that "these technologies conceal instances of 'our' brutality, enacted in the name of peace, reconciliation, and the rule of law, while paradoxically reinscribing violence and injury through the process of humanizing the other."[28] Atanasoski interrogates the violence inherent in the process of humanizing the other in the refugee camp. She shows that humanitarianism and violence are not mutually exclusive but reinforce each other to legitimize the use of violence to "save" the colonized other from conditions that were made possible by colonialism in the first place.

A UNHCR document titled "Guidelines for Estimating Food and Nutritional Needs in Emergencies" reveals the violence of humanitarianism and the ways in which refugee bodies are policed by the UNHCR: "Until now, [the World Food Program] and UNHCR have used a reference value of 1,900 kilocalories per person per day for designing emergency rations. This planning figure, which was endorsed by the 1988 Conference 'Nutrition in Times of Disaster,' is based on the needs of a 'typical' sedentary population with a normal demographic distribution and an assumed physical activity level of 45 percent above the Basal Metabolic Rate."[29] This UNHCR document illuminates the restrictions placed on refugee lives and the policing of refugee bodies. The people who are tasked with creating the 1,900-calorie limitation are not refugees; yet these same people are given the power to create guidelines for refugee food intake. The absence of refugee input in the creation of refugee policies illuminates the clear power imbalance between refugees and humanitarian workers. I interviewed Halwa Hamdi, a Somali refugee residing in San Diego, about the calorie restrictions: "The camp officials gave us less food than we needed to survive, especially since many of us had large families. How could they expect us to live on so little food? Would the camp officials give their families the same food rations? I think not."[30] The calorie restrictions imposed on Somali refugees are guided by the belief that refugees are sedentary, which is false because refugees devote significant time to physical activities such as collecting wood and water. The refugee camp functions like a prison because the camp is a site where people's lives are wholly organized and regimented by an external force.

Yet, when I lived in Dadaab as a child, it was the only home I knew. Along with my siblings and other children, I spent my days playing soccer. To us Dadaab did not feel like a prison, but there were moments that reminded us of our constrained conditions. I distinctly remember a day when Kenyan school children walked by the camp and in Swahili called us dirty refugees. We were kept behind the barbed wire fence while the Kenyan children were free to roam. This was the moment I realized that our circumstances were different from other children outside the refugee camp. The Kenyan school children were wearing bright and colorful uniforms, while we wore dirty and ripped clothing. They wore shoes, and we went barefoot as our feet navigated a harsh terrain with a perpetual threat of jigger bug infestation. Despite the bleakness of the refugee camp, we found ways to experience joy.

Like my own experiences, other Somali refugees found ways to experience joy and exercise agency in the camp despite the restrictions imposed on refugee movement and freedom. One way in which refugees exercised agency is by explicitly withholding information from the police to aid other refugees in escaping police violence. Refugees are keenly aware that control over information is a central mechanism through which police power operates. Somali refugees refused to cooperate with the police to frustrate the police's capacity to surveil them. Cawo spent five years in the camps and vividly remembers her encounters with the Kenyan police. Explaining the rationale behind refugees deceiving the

Kenyan police, she says, "We lied to the Kenyan police to protect each other; they cannot be trusted, so we didn't tell them anything."[31] Cawo's words—"they cannot be trusted"—reflect the trust that was broken because the Kenyan police demonstrated complete disregard for the lives of Somali refugees, who had to become accountable to each other in finding ways to escape police surveillance. Somali refugees did this by sharing information with each other on effective methods for navigating police violence. They congregated in each other's homes to share information about upcoming police raids. By meeting in each other's homes, Somali refugees built a form of community knowledge that was used to evade police raids. This community knowledge highlights the significance of a Somali refugee epistemology. My mother relayed to me one evening that "life in the refugee camp was not that bad; we had community. There was always someone there to help you and share food and knowledge. Life in America is lonely: you have to do everything by yourself, [and] there is not as much community here." My mother's comment refutes the idea that refugees' lives improve in the United States; instead, life is often more difficult due to the loneliness endemic to individualized households. Moreover, this statement rejects American individualism and contrasts it with the intricate community networks that sustained Somali refugees through the experience of war and the carcerality of the refugee camp.

These community-based networks among Somali refugees flourished as refugees shared food, shelter, and information with each other. This network of information circulated by Somali refugees is based on a chain of knowledge, where certain refugees who had recent encounters with police relay that information to other refugees. By circulating this information, Somali refugees helped other refugees learn critical details about individual police officers, including their routes and dispositions. The stories Somali refugees told each other about the police became an essential tool for survival. Storytelling served both as an epistemological basis for refugee identity and as a practical tool for circumventing police violence.

Somali refugees also devised unique strategies for engaging with humanitarian workers. Refugees employed what James Scott has called "public transcripts" to shift the power imbalance between refugees and humanitarian workers.[32] Public transcripts are the public displays of docility performed by the oppressed, which, upon closer inspection, reveal subtle forms of resistance. Somali refugees presented a public image of subservience to gain additional resources necessary for life in the camps. Somali refugees' performance of subservience became a way to derive agency and accumulate resources for their families.

Omar is a Somali taxicab driver in City Heights who had many stories about his time in the Dadaab refugee camp. Omar described how refugees mobilize stereotypes about themselves to outmaneuver camp officials. He revealed that "the refugee camp officer was always condescending to us, so we would hide some of our daily rations so that we could get more later. They thought we were stupid, but we only played dumb, so, in the end, they were the ones that were fooled."[33] Refugees are complex subjects who perform docility in the face of state power; Omar's story also underscores the ingenuity displayed by Somali refugees.

Scott's analytic of public transcripts is useful here because it shows that the greater the power differential between the oppressors and the oppressed, the thicker the mask of docility. Aisha Hassan, who spent three years in Dadaab, relayed that aid workers would routinely lord their power over refugees. In *Scenes of*

Subjection, Saidiya Hartman argues that "the exercise of power [is] inseparable from its display."[34] Yet Somali refugees' resistance to power in the camps often takes a subtle form and is separate from its display.

Therefore, it is critical to emphasize the outward performance of docility, or what Hartman terms the "simulation of compliance," rather than the fact of it.[35] Privately, Somali refugees would criticize aid workers who they believed derided refugees in the camp. Omar shared that "we would always make fun of the UNHCR workers, because they always looked at us like we were dirty and beneath them, so we did the same back to them."[36] In other words, Somalis were intimately aware of the perception held by some UNHCR workers that refugees could not be trusted, and they responded by privately and at times publicly mocking aid workers. Scott describes this phenomenon as follows: "The theater of power can, by artful practice, become an actual political resource of subordinates. Thus, we get the wrong impression, I think, if we visualize actors perpetually wearing fake smiles and moving with the reluctance of a chain gang. To do so is to see the performance as totally determined from above and miss the agency of the actor in appropriating the performance for his own ends."[37] The appearance of docility on the part of the oppressed is not a marker of powerlessness, according to Scott; rather, it is one of the limited tools employed by the oppressed to resist domination. Somali refugees use public displays of docility to navigate the uneven power relations inherent in the structure of the refugee camp, where their input is rarely solicited in making the executive decisions that affect their lives. These subtle forms of refugee resistance disrupt the dominant narrative of refugees as helpless subjects. Scott's notion of infrapolitics provides a conceptual framework for grasping the moments in which refugees manipulate the bureaucracy of the refugee camp in their favor.

Another manifestation of infrapolitics is Somali refugees' mobilization of flexible kinship strategies. For example, Somali refugees sometimes claim spouses to whom they are not married to increase the likelihood of getting approved for resettlement. The United States' refugee resettlement policies are organized around the idealization of the heteronormative family; hence, a family comprising a married mother and father with children born from that union is much more likely to be approved for resettlement.[38] Therefore, the composition of Somali refugee families is heavily policed and surveilled by the camp officials. Somalis are keenly aware of these carceral practices and have utilized various techniques to circumvent these heteronormative refugee resettlement policies to increase their chances of being selected for resettlement. Safia, a Somali refugee activist, highlights the intricacies of this practice:

> In Dadaab we noticed that single mothers were not getting resettlement. Many of them would get rejected for refugee resettlement before the interview stage. But people with traditional families such as a married husband and wife with children would be much more likely to get resettlement. So, people came up with creative ways to improve their chances, like creating fake marriages, buying a marriage certificate so that a single mother could get a better chance at resettlement. The mother would pay money to a man who would pretend to be her husband, and once they both entered the US, they would divorce after a couple of years.[39]

The creative strategies highlighted by Safia are part of the repertoires that have helped numerous refugee families. Many of these families would not have been resettled without adopting these flexible kinship strategies. UNHCR officials altered their refugee resettlement policies because of Somali refugees' reliance on what the UNHCR terms "family composition fraud"; in effect, the UNHCR changed its policies in response to Somali refugees' creative tactics. The UNHCR document "Managing Resettlement Effectively" details the UN's response to these refugee repertoires:

> Family composition fraud is one of the areas where misrepresentation or fraud is most likely to be committed. The definition of a family is culturally specific, and care must be taken to accurately record real relationships, as misrepresentation may not have a fraudulent intent. However, family composition fraud may involve marriages of convenience; fictitious relationships, such as when distant relatives are claimed as sons and daughters; adding fictitious family members; substituting children, which may occur for money or under duress; or "losing" or hiding a family member to get an improved chance at resettlement.[40]

As this document reveals, the UNHCR is aware that the term *family* is culturally specific but continues to police the myriad ways that Somali refugees create families. Michel Foucault's theory that power is informed by resistance and that "this resistance is never in a position of exteriority to power" illuminates the reciprocal relationship between Somali refugees' life-sustaining practices and the bureaucracy of the UNHCR.[41] In response to these life-sustaining practices, the UNHCR adopted a new policy that instructed case workers to interview each member of a refugee family to verify their familial relationship.

A UN document titled "Interviewing Applicants for Refugee Status" highlights this new approach, which directs UN interviewers to "assess the applicant's story and credibility in connection with the principles and criteria for determination of refugee status. This requires that the applicant's story be carefully documented and cross-checked."[42] In the context of the bureaucracy of refugee resettlement, refugee stories are a site of legal and political contestation. Therefore, telling the *correct* story can mean the difference between getting refugee status or living without the benefits that come with being legally recognized as a refugee. Refugees are recommended for resettlement based on a set of criteria that judge their vulnerability to historical and ongoing violence because of their ethnic identity. Therefore, refugees whose suffering is not deemed "sufficient" by the interviewers are rejected for resettlement. Moreover, the legal criteria for attaining legal recognition as refugees ignore gender-based violence. As a result of this arbitrary and strict criterion, only 1 percent of refugees are ever resettled.[43]

Children are often interviewed separately from their parents to authenticate the validity of their parent's marriage as well as the children's relationship to their parents. During my family's interview process, my younger sister, who was five at the time, was interviewed alone to verify that my family was indeed related. As a response to these new UNHCR policies, Somali refugee families began coaching their children to ensure that they provided the "correct" answers to refugee resettlement agents. This intricate dance between UNHCR agents and refugees highlights the changing and complex interplay between power and resistance. In 2021, the Kenyan state began criminalizing the refugee repertoires by imposing jail time on any refugee that "knowingly and willfully enters into a marriage for the sole purpose of assisting another refugee to obtain any of the benefits conferred by this Act."[44] According to this act, the creative, life-sustaining strategies Somali refugees developed to help each other navigate the burdensome and hostile refugee apparatuses in Kenya are criminalized and policed by the state. In the face of the state's increased surveillance of the refugee repertoires, Somali refugees continue to invent new ways to subvert a legal and political system that works against their needs by design. The refugee repertoires that developed out of the carceral refugee camp have emerged as forms of community knowledge and are shared with other refugees through stories. Somali refugees also employ this community knowledge to escape the clutches of state surveillance in the United States.

City Heights and Dadaab, here juxtaposed, are two sites that instrumentalize surveillance apparatuses to restrict the movements of Somali refugees. For example, Somali refugees in Dadaab are required to carry identification cards whenever they leave the camps. In City Heights, Somali youths are required to carry identification to walk the streets at night. Somali youths in City Heights are prohibited from traveling at night due to police enforcement of curfew laws.[45] Somali refugees have had to navigate the carceral state from Kenya to San Diego, all the while developing tools to resist the carceral state through the refugee repertoire.

Conclusion

Somali refugees have developed a complex repertoire of resistance in response to the militarized violence of the Somali civil war and the carceral space of the refugee camp. In these sites, Somali refugees developed tools to survive state violence and seek resettlement. In many of my interviews, resistance to state violence emerged as a common theme that governed the Somali refugee experience across both space and time. In chapter 1, I interrogated the relationship between humanitarianism and militarism by investigating the US military's 1992 peacekeeping mission in Somalia, Operation Restore Hope. In this chapter, I examined the convergence between humanitarianism and policing in the Dadaab refugee camp. Somalis moved through various militarized and carceral spaces, all the while developing tools to survive.

Somalis responded to the collapse of the Somali state by creating networks of support that superseded the state. The collapse of the Somali state is the condition of possibility for the Somali refugee repertoire. The refugee repertoire develops from the reciprocal relationship between power and resistance. Somali refugees invented creative methods to share information, food, and housing, as well as ingenious ways to circumvent state violence. In the absence of a robust welfare state in both Kenya and the United States, Somali refugees continuously and meticulously developed life-sustaining practices. In the Dadaab refugee camp, Somalis developed effective and intricate survival strategies rooted in shared experiences of violence and survival. Somalis brought these practices with them to San Diego, as they encountered institutional racism in every sector of American society. Somali refugees' experiences with state violence provide insight into our increasingly carceral and militarized state and how Black immigrant communities can survive and thrive in spite of it.

3 Confronting Anti-Black Racism

Militarized Policing in San Diego

The objective of this chapter is to detail Somali refugee experiences with militarized policing in San Diego. There is a dearth of projects that interrogate the ways in which militarism informs and shapes contemporary police practices. Moreover, scholarship on policing rarely focuses on the experiences of refugees. By adopting a Critical Refugee Studies approach, I argue that the Somali refugee exodus is conditioned by US militarism and therefore reveals the intersections between US militarism and refugees.

Somali refugees' experiences with both US militarized violence abroad and police violence domestically highlight the increasingly intimate relationship between the US military and police. The San Diego Police Department's deployment of SWAT teams serves as a case study to analyze police militarization. San Diego is an epicenter of US militarism, and the San Diego police routinely hire military veterans into its police force. Moreover, the San Diego police have close ties to the military bases scattered all over the city. Therefore, San Diego is a premier site to study the national trend of police militarization. I also investigate the role of community policing in extending the reach of the carceral state into the lives and community spaces of Somali refugees. Moreover, San

Diego has also emerged as a city where Somali refugees have taken prominent roles in the Black Lives Matter movement to address the related effects of military violence and police violence on the lives and bodies of Black people.

Coming to San Diego

In the early 1990s, San Diego, California, became a popular destination for Somali refugees leaving Dadaab, Kenya.[1] The US State Department chose to resettle Somali refugees in the City Heights neighborhood of San Diego because the city possesses a high concentration of refugee resettlement organizations.[2] More refugees were resettled in San Diego in February 2017 than in any other region of California. In 2016, California accepted more refugees than any other state in the country.[3] San Diego has a plethora of nonprofit organizations that are dedicated to helping refugees, such as the International Rescue Committee.[4] In the fall of 2017, the California Department of Social Services produced a chart that details refugee arrivals to California by region.

According to this dataset, San Diego accepts more refugees than any other city in California, and by a large margin. Within the city of San Diego, City Heights represents a local manifestation of the global circuits of US imperialism. Three of the largest refugee communities in San Diego—Somali, Iraqi, and Vietnamese—arrived in San Diego as a result of US wars in their homelands. The vibrant and interconnected refugee community in City Heights provides a counter-map of US imperialism and its trail of devastation. By analyzing the interconnected histories of US imperialism in Somalia, Vietnam, and Iraq, I expose its role in producing refugee crises globally. I make the argument that the US military went to Somalia long before Somalis came to the United States.

US militarism created the conditions of possibility for the Somali refugee crisis. In San Diego, Somali refugees encountered a new yet familiar form of militarized violence. The city of San Diego—home to the Marine Corps base Camp Pendleton and to Naval Base San Diego, one of the largest bases of the US Navy—is a militarized space. The University of California, San Diego, also produces drone research, and fighter jets regularly fly across the San Diego sky.[5] As a consequence, Somali refugees escaped militarized violence in Somalia only to encounter the strong military presence in San Diego and the domestic form of militarized policing. In City Heights this militarism took the form of SWAT teams.

It was in the context of increased state violence directed at Black communities that the first wave of Somali refugees arrived in City Heights in 1993.[6] In the early 1990s news media, Somalis were racialized and represented as dangerous refugees rather than as people in need of humanitarian aid. A 1994 news article from the *San Diego Union-Tribune* highlights how Somalia is represented as a space imbued with irrational violence, ruled by warlords, and devoid of any political and historical complexity. According to the article, "Officer Patty Clayton said the anti-police attitude among youths was a throwback to life in their homeland, places such as Somalia, Ethiopia, Sudan, where anybody in a uniform was to be feared. Police were corrupt and violent. Ditto the military. Warlords ruled."[7] Officer Clayton's statement draws from colonial discourses of Africans, produced by Western observers, as violent "savages." Officer Clayton assumed that violence and corruption are natural to Africa, eliding the long history of colonial violence directed at Africans. Moreover, these colonial discourses depicting

Africans as savages continue to be promoted by journalists and film producers. This discourse of Somali savagery is clearly present in the 2013 film *Captain Phillips*.[8] In this film Somali pirates are portrayed "as savages—as oafs who continuously fall for the captain's tricks and deceptions."[9] Depictions of Somalis as savages in films like *Captain Phillips* are utilized to justify US military presence in Somalia.

Negotiating Blackness

The pathologizing of Blackness has a distinct history in relation to immigrant communities. According to segmented assimilation theory, Black immigrants are trapped in poverty because they adopt the cultural values of poor Black people.[10] The segmented assimilation framework draws from the culture-of-poverty thesis popularized by sociologist Patrick Moynihan. Culture-of-poverty discourses gained traction in government institutions in the 1960s and 1970s. Moynihan produced an (in)famous report in 1965 titled *The Negro Family: The Case for National Action*.[11] In this report Moynihan argues that Black culture is the root cause of poverty in Black communities. The Blackness-as-pathology framework influenced public policies regarding the Black community.

Segmented assimilation theory is rooted in the claim that Black immigrants can access upward mobility by adopting the values of the white middle class and that, conversely, they experience downward mobility by associating with working-class African Americans.[12] I counter this framework by arguing that Somali refugee youths have become politicized out of solidarity with African Americans in the Black Lives Matter movement and share the goal of police abolition. Somali refugee activists have argued that they draw from the long legacy of African American resistance to state violence in negotiating their own positionality and Blackness.

A Somali activist named Idil explains to me what it means to be Black in America:

> I feel like the chains have never been broken from Black people in this country, whether you're someone who is an immigrant or someone who's a multigenerational Black diaspora person. It is something that is just, as you come into this country, you are definitely one of those. If you're a Black person, you are definitely a person with a target or chains and shackles and being able to envision a way to take away that target, take away the shackle.[13]

The repeated references to "chains" in this statement represent the afterlives of slavery that conditions so much of Black life in the United States. Saidiya Hartman characterizes the afterlife of slavery as "skewed life chances, limited access to health and education, premature death, incarceration, and impoverishment."[14] One manifestation of the afterlife of slavery is policing, which has its roots in slave patrols and continues to structure Black life.

It is within this context that Somali refugees navigate the United States as Black immigrants. Due to the institutionalization of anti-Black racism in the United States, Somali refugees do not have the capacity to be assimilated into white culture as previous generations of immigrants (like the Irish) were after experiencing systematic discrimination and racism.[15] A 2018 report stated that about 54 percent of Somalis live below the poverty line.[16] This high rate of poverty is also conditioned by Somali refugees' experiences with housing segregation, education inequities, and discrimination in the employment sector. Moreover, since 2006, 25 percent of

African immigrants have come to the United States as refugees, whereas refugees make up 7 percent of the total US immigrant population. A larger share of African immigrants came to the United States as refugees, and this population is generally poorer and has fewer resources. According to a report by the Migration Policy Institute, "Five refugee source countries—Ethiopia, Somalia, Liberia, Sudan and Eritrea—together accounted for 30 percent of all Black African immigrants in 2009."[17] Therefore, Somali refugees are part of the shift in African immigration brought about by the influx of African refugees. African refugees not only come to the United States with limited resources but are also often resettled in under-resourced and over-policed neighborhoods, thus creating generations of cyclical poverty. As of 2007, only 7 percent of Somalis had a college degree, which is significantly below the US average of 27 percent.[18] This startling statistic reveals how Somali refugees' resettlements into under-resourced neighborhoods leads to low levels of access to college and thereby limits Somali refugees to low-wage jobs.

Somali refugees experience the myriad forms of anti-Black racism that mark the Black experience in the United States, including residential segregation, criminalization, and unequal access to quality education. The first generation of Somali refugees to the United States did not have a context for understanding the nuances of anti-Black racism in the United States, and some even tried to distance themselves from Blackness. A Somali activist named Suada explains how her aunts navigated Blackness: "And so, for example, this idea that, you know, we're not Black . . . we're Somali, but we're not like them, and that was an attitude that like I've heard from her, from my aunties, from other women in the community, elder women."[19] This idea that we are not "like them" is a means for the first generation of Somali refugees to distance themselves from African Americans. Yet, for Somali youths, distancing themselves from Blackness does not offer any reprieve from police violence and racial profiling because Somalis experience heightened levels of surveillance at the hands of the state.

Suada explained to her mother that what happened to Trayvon Martin could and does happen to Somali youths. Suada told her mother, "This is us, this is all of us; like, we're all in this together," meaning that vulnerability to police violence is a fate shared by the broader Black diaspora regardless of ethnic or national differences. This was clearly demonstrated by the police shooting of a Somali man, Dolal Idd, months after police in Minneapolis killed George Floyd.[20] Moreover, second-generation Somali refugees like Suada realized that Blackness was not the main issue plaguing the Somali community, but rather the structural inequities rooted in anti-Black racism, such as racial profiling and unequal access to housing and education.

The 2015 trial of George Zimmerman was a critical moment in the politicization of Somali refugee youths. Suada remembers this moment well: "I was fifteen years old when Trayvon Martin was killed, was murdered by George Zimmerman, and when the Black Lives Matter movement really came to the forefront. . . . And, you know, throwing myself into that, you know, wanting so desperately to be a part of Black Lives Matter and wanting to be part of the groundbreaking work that they were doing."[21] In the BLM movement, young Somali refugees worked together with African Americans toward the goal of police abolition. This solidarity between African Americans and Somali refugees during the BLM protests in San Diego and Minneapolis challenges the scholarly and media representations of perpetual conflict between African immigrants and African Americans.[22] The 2015 BLM movement and the summer 2020 BLM protests politicized many young Somali refugees around the issue of police brutality.[23] The BLM protests gave voice to Somali refugees' routine experiences with racial profiling and hostile encounters with the police. Jama, a Somali activist, says that the police have a way of "making us feel like we're dangerous, making us feel like we're criminals."[24]

Like the scholars who employ segmented assimilation theory, police claimed that young Somalis were turning to crime because they were associating with other Black youths. Hamza, a Somali refugee intimately familiar with the belief that Somali refugees could achieve "whiteness" by rejecting Blackness, says that "the cops in the afterschool program would tell us that we have to stop acting like the Black kids because we would end up dead or in jail if we started acting like, talking like, or dressing like the other Black kids in City Heights." Hamza also states that "one of the cops then said: 'Well, they are Africans; we can't teach savages to be civilized.'"[25] In Hamza's retelling of this experience, the police use the culture-of-poverty ideology to demonize Blackness.

Somali youths' experiences in City Heights sit at the intersection between the historical racialization of Black Americans as criminals and the racialization of Africans as "savages." The racialization of Blackness travels across space and time, yet the racialization of Blackness is also geographically specific, as the differing racialization of Somalis in Kenya and San Diego indicates. Moreover, for Somali youths, Blackness is a political identity as well as a racial identity. Stuart Hall has observed how Blackness became "a way of referencing the common experience of racism and marginalization in Britain and came to provide the organizing category of a new politics of resistance, among groups and communities with, in fact, very different histories, traditions, and ethnic identities."[26] Similarly, during the BLM movement in the summer of 2020, Somali refugees in San Diego organized with a diversity of Black people to develop a politics of resistance over their shared experiences with police brutally that cut across ethnic and national divides within the broader Black community. During these BLM protests, young Somali refugees viewed Blackness as a site of resistance and a means to build solidarity with African Americans and other African youths around issues of police violence and anti-Blackness writ large.

Criminalizing Blackness

A June 2005 article in the *San Diego Union-Tribune* sheds light on the racialization of African youths as criminals in San Diego. The article claims that "crime among the African youths on San Diego streets was escalating. Gangs were proliferating. Burglaries, vandalism, assaults, and truancies were becoming the norm."[27] This particular story mobilized white fears of Black youths and was subsequently taken up by the state as a rationale for the enforcement of curfew laws. The creation of curfew laws made Somali youths more vulnerable to police surveillance.[28] Nasir, a Somali college student, explains, "A lot of my friends have been harassed and arrested by police. We think that because there is a large number of cops patrolling City Heights . . . we are always getting pulled over by police."[29] According to a 2023 KPBS article, "San Diego police made 141 curfew arrests last year, according to their own records, mostly of Black and Latino youth."[30] The oversaturation of images of "Black on Black violence" and gang warfare in local news outlets was taken up by the state government to legitimize the heightened police presence that Nasir references. The *San Diego Union-Tribune* and other media outlets transformed Black rage over deteriorating social conditions into the threat, and police violence was cast as the solution to this perceived threat.

Mobilizing to critique police violence due to the state's unwillingness to address institutional racism, Somali youths produce counternarratives that challenge the narrative of Black criminality. They claim instead that the police are criminals. Young Somali activists shed light on the state's relegation of Black people to premature death through the institutionalization of inequality in the health care, housing, and criminal justice systems. Safia, a Somali refugee activist, declares: "Us Somali people in City Heights, we are not committing crimes—this is our neighborhood, why would we destroy it? The police are lying; they do not make me feel safe; they scare me. I feel safer in City Heights than I do in La Jolla where all the rich white people live."[31] In this incisive analysis, Safia locates police brutality, rather than Black pathology, as the root cause of state violence. Her interrogation of state violence echoes Afropessimist Frank Wilderson, who claims that Blackness is "always already criminalized in the collective unconscious."[32] Safia's assertion also mirrors Dorothy Roberts's insistence that the "unconscious association between Blacks and crime is so powerful that it supersedes reality: it predisposes whites to literally see Black people as criminals. Their skin marks Blacks as visibly lawless."[33] Roberts shows that the rhetoric of "law and order" is premised on the subjugation of Black life. Moreover, the significant state resources earmarked for law enforcement due to the 1994 crime bill reveal the political currency the law-and-order rhetoric grants police.[34]

The BLM movement linked the most violent and visible manifestation of policing—the murder of Black people by police—to the racial disparities built into the criminal (in)justice system. Police brutality is not an aberration from the normal execution of police duties; rather, it is central to the functioning of police. According to a 2017 Department of Justice investigation of the Chicago Police Department, "We, in consultation with several active law enforcement experts, found that CPD officers engage in a pattern or practice of using force, including deadly force, that is unreasonable. We found further that CPD officers' force practices unnecessarily endanger themselves and others and result in unnecessary and avoidable shootings and other uses of force."[35] This Department of Justice investigation found that the use of deadly force was normalized within the Chicago police. The BLM movement unsettles the naturalization of police violence by bringing national attention to police murders of Black people.[36] BLM disrupts the normal functioning of policing, which in many cities is premised on violating Black bodies.

Police murders of Black people have historically been represented as isolated incidents by both the police and media outlets, but in the age of social media, news of the deaths of Black people at the hands of the police is instantly available to people around the world. Yasmin, a Somali refugee, explains the visceral reaction she has to viewing police murders of Black people on social media: "Seeing all the images of Black people being killed by police on my Facebook page, Twitter, and CNN really inspired be to become an activist. I couldn't take seeing all this senseless death, so I decided to do something about it. It's the same story with a lot of my fellow activists, especially the young ones who were never really interested in activism [but] became Twitter activists."[37] Yasmin reveals that in the summer of 2020 the circulation of images of Black death on social media was traumatizing for her, as she was inundated with the spectacle of Black suffering. In *Scenes of Subjection*, Saidiya Hartman argues that these spectacles of Black suffering create a pornography of Black pain that links Blackness to suffering.[38] According to Yasmin, the counternarratives provided by BLM activists served as a catalyst for her activism and interrupted the paralysis she felt with viewing so much Black death in the news.

Social media forums such as "Black Twitter" have been critical spaces for BLM activists, because it is in these spaces that activists produce counternarratives to the ones being furnished by news media outlets. Barbara Ransby's *Making All Black Lives Matter* argues that "Twitter in particular has become a special kind of public square for African Americans, who use the medium in a higher concentration than their white counterparts—so much so that the Black online communities that follow, engage, and retweet one another are sometimes referred to as 'Black Twitter.'"[39] Black Twitter activists provide a counternarrative to the one provided by the news media by shifting the focus from Black criminality to police injustice. Somali youths have also taken up Twitter as a means to spotlight police murders of Somalis. Aisha, a Somali activist, says, "We went on Twitter to let people know that Minneapolis police had also killed Somali man Dolal Idd months after the police murder of George Floyd."[40] The police murder of Dolal Idd on December 3, 2020, received scant media attention and even less attention from BLM activists outside of the Somali community.[41] Therefore, Somali activists joined BLM activists to call attention to the violence Black immigrants and refugees experience at the hands of the police. Somali refugees also experience policing from other state agents besides law enforcement, such as Section 8 housing officials, who make unannounced visits to people's houses, and representatives of welfare agencies.

Therefore, policing is an entire apparatus that can be deployed by shop owners, social workers, teachers, security guards, and individuals to discipline Black people. During my interviews, Somali youths recounted their experiences with being "policed" in City Heights. Abdikareem, a Somali refugee youth who resides in City Heights, says that store clerks at the local 7-Eleven often follow him from aisle to aisle. With a quiet yet determined rage, Abdikareem says, "I hate going to the 7-Eleven because the white clerk is always messing with me, and he called the cops on me one time. He hates me because I'm Black."[42] Abdikareem's story reveals the myriad ways Black people are surveilled in this country. The white clerk's deployment of the police is both a mundane and spectacular instantiation of state violence. Abdi's declaration that "he hates me because I'm Black" draws attention to the hypervisibility of Blackness in public spaces and the state terror to which this hypervisibility exposes Black people. The police read Black subjects as physical manifestations of criminality and respond to the presence of Black people with violence. Yet regardless of how individual Somalis identify, as the experiences of Somali youths highlight, Somalis are racialized as Black and criminalized by state agents.

In *The Condemnation of Blackness*, Khalil Gibran Muhammad shows how the criminalization of Blackness makes Black people vulnerable to state surveillance without the presumption of innocence.[43] According to Frantz Fanon, in his classic *Black Skin, White Masks*, the Black body is distorted by the white gaze: "My body was returned to me spread-eagled, disjointed, redone, draped in mourning on this white winter's day."[44] Somali refugee youths have found ways to challenge the White gaze and its distorting impact by using cell phones to turn the gaze back.

Counter-Technologies of Policing

Somali youths also developed their own technology to counteract this carceral technology. To introduce accountability, these young Somalis film police—the belief being that officers will be less likely to commit violence if taped. By filming police assaults and disseminating it on social media, Somali youths have exposed the dark underbelly of policing in America. Ilyas explains Somali youths' rationale for utilizing these counter-technologies: "We take out our cameras to record police because if we don't, they will attack the person and beat them. By recording them, they will be more afraid to do that kind of stuff."[45] Ilyas's story indicates that Somali refugees are not passive in the face of state violence; their counter-technologies against police surveillance draw from the long history of Black resistance to police violence. In the 1960s, the Black Panther Party created a similar program to observe police officers during routine police stops. Historian Ashley Farmer writes that "early Panther members would roam around observing police, challenging their treatment of black detainees, and loudly reciting the penal code so that both the police and observers could hear."[46]

Somali youths draw from this history by creating their own database of police officers who have been a source of danger for Somali youths. As knowledge of the database spread through word of mouth, young Somali refugees were building a form of community knowledge. Youth-led counter-policing strategies would become even more important as the San Diego police continued to militarize. According to a 2021 *San Diego Union-Tribune* news article, "Some protesters and social justice advocates have criticized San Diego for having its officers wear tactical gear during protests and for using 'tanks' to intimidate protesters."[47] The San Diego police deployed militarized weapons to intimidate BLM protesters. Therefore, just as activists respond to the strategies of the police, so too do police respond, often with militarized violence, to the strategies of activists. The San Diego police can mobilize a tank against predominantly Black activists by mobilizing the discourse of Black criminality to racialize Black people as threats.

I borrow from the work of Simone Browne to interrogate the role that the news media play in normalizing police violence. In her discussion of the police assault on Rodney King, Browne contends that "police violence is not read as violence; rather, the racially saturated field of visibility fixed and framed Rodney King and read his actions, as recorded by Holliday, as that danger from which whiteness must be protected."[48] Somali refugee experiences with racial profiling shed light on the material impacts of this propagation of Black criminality in the news media. Numerous Somali youths shared stories of their experiences with racial profiling at the hands of the San Diego police. Mohamed, a Somali college student, states that he had recently been harassed by police for loitering. He says, "We didn't do nothing. The police mess with us for just standing around."[49] Loitering laws were created to protect property at the expense of Black mobility. This impetus to protect property at the expense of Black lives is disturbing, considering Black lives used to be white property in this nation. During the BLM protests in the summer of 2020, there was a focus on the property damage linked to BLM protesters. This concern for damaged property underscores how the state values property more than Black lives. An NBC 7 San Diego news story highlights BLM protesters' destruction of property: "Local tensions erupted in the large protest on May 30, which saw protesters take over Interstate 8 and, later, local shopping centers, where several local businesses were eventually looted, as was a nearby Vons."[50] In this news article, BLM protesters are portrayed as threats to private property, while police are portrayed as protectors of private property. Cheryl Harris explains how this association of whiteness with property arose: "The origins of whiteness as property lie in the parallel systems of domination of Black and Native American peoples out of which were created racially contingent forms of property and property rights."[51] Therefore, the destruction of property is metaphorically an assault on whiteness. George Lipsitz argues that whiteness is "property" and that "the possessive investment in whiteness always emerges from a fused sensibility drawing on many sources at once—on anti-black racism to be sure, but also on the legacies of racialization theft by federal, state, and local policies toward Native Americans, Asian Americans, Mexican Americans, and other groups designated by whites as 'racially other.'"[52] Police therefore function to protect white property and maintain a racist and unequal social order. This social order is defended by an increasingly militarized police force.

Special Weapons and Tactics Teams: Militarized Police in San Diego

Somali refugees experience the most militarized violence through the action of SWAT teams within the San Diego Police Department (SDPD). According to San Diego SWAT commanding officer Mark Saunders, "We now have one of the largest SWAT units in the country, because we never want to see an officer or anyone else bleeding out. We want to be able to get them out of harm's way, and out of the hot zone, so medics can help them right away."[53] It is not surprising that San Diego has one of the largest SWAT teams because

San Diego is a militarized city with a total of seven military bases.[54] One officer in San Diego's SWAT team said, "I know a lot of people think we're real militaristic, but we're not. Most of the stuff we use the BearCat [armored vehicle] for is protection purposes only."[55] The use of a BearCat for protection begs the question: Protection from whom? In the case of San Diego, the police department claims the use of military equipment is justified in communities they deem most threating—namely, those of immigrants, activists, Black, poor, and working-class people.

In the 1990s, SWAT teams in San Diego were often deployed to deliver search warrants for low-level drug offenses. According to a report from the Council on Criminal Justice's Task Force on Policing, "The most common use of SWAT teams was to execute search warrants, with 91 percent of all SWAT deployments involving execution of a search warrant and 68 percent involving forcible entry."[56] For the Somali refugees who fled the violence of war in Somalia, the sight of militarized police breaking down doors is a haunting reminder of their previous encounters with US militarism in their own country. Radley Balko writes that "publications like Larry Flynt's *SWAT* magazine feature ads that emphasize knocking heads and kicking ass, and print articles with headlines like 'Go for the Throat' and 'Warrior Mindset.'"[57] According to this "warrior mindset," the police are warriors, and communities of color are the enemies.

Tahim is a longtime resident of City Heights who first arrived as a refugee in San Diego in 1995. He shares a story regarding the actions of the SDPD's SWAT teams: "It seemed like every night there would be a SWAT team breaking down doors and arresting people in our neighborhood. They would often use armored trucks with battering rams just to get into one guy's apartment." The

[84] CONFRONTING ANTI-BLACK RACISM

SWAT teams Tahim references were a part of the Gang Suppression Unit (GSU), which was known for its aggressive tactics.

The creation of the GSU was justified by the so-called War on Drugs, and this unit has a well-documented track record of using excessive force against Black communities. Tahim remembers the terror the GSU inflicted on Somali youths: "The gang prevention unit thought all Black kids were gang members. They were crazy and would come by every day to check our pockets and shove us against the wall. They would sometimes even call our houses and threaten us with arrest."[58] Tahim's recollection of the GSU is confirmed by a description quoted in a *Voice of San Diego* article, which sheds light on the workings of this unit: "'The gang suppression team, they roll like a mob,' said Lincoln Park Minister Hugh Muhammad at the hearing. . . . 'They roll deep. They roll three, four, five cars,' Muhammad said. 'They're very disrespectful. Matter of fact, in my opinion, sometimes they think they're above reproach.'"[59]

In the quote above, Muhammad's likening of the police to a "mob" is a counternarrative that indicts the criminality of state agents who regularly violate Black bodies. SWAT teams were often deployed to City Heights under "no-knock" policies. No-knock warrants are issued with the stipulation that police officers do not need to knock or identify themselves before entering someone's house.[60] These warrants were often issued for drug-related searches. Some of the refugees I interviewed experienced the terror of police officers breaking down their doors without knocking or identifying themselves as police. Out of all people I interviewed, Barsanji has the most experience with no-knock warrants and the detrimental impacts of over-policing on the Somali refugee community.

Barsanji has lived in City Heights for twenty years and is active in the Somali refugee community. I asked him about his experiences with SWAT teams in San Diego, and he said his experiences eerily mirrored the Somali civil war and the terror of militarized violence. According to Barsanji, "It seemed like every day that another person in our apartment complex would have their doors broken down in the middle of the night by SWAT teams. They entered people's houses by throwing flash grenades, scaring everyone inside. The worst part of it was that they would never repair the damage they did, so people had to live with broken doors and windows."[61] Victims of police violence must live with the daily reminders of the original scene of violence—these are lingering emotional, physical, and material impacts. In Barsanji's story, the broken door and windows provide a physical reminder of the threat of indiscriminate state violence. The visual evidence of state violence does not disappear when the police disappear; rather, it is in the scene of destruction that the presence/absence of the police is most clearly demarcated. Moreover, Somali refugees fled the violence of their home country hoping to find sanctuary in the United States, but instead they have been met with state-sanctioned violence in the form of militarized policing.

In addition to the visual, there are also sonic dimensions to police violence, to which the residents of City Heights are clearly attuned. To live in City Heights is to become accustomed to the sound of police sirens. For the recently resettled Somali refugee community, the sound of police sirens echoed the sounds of war. During the Somali civil war, the noises of militarized violence inundated the streets of Mogadishu. The memories of war return as police sirens flood the streets of City Heights. Ayaan, a Somali resident from City Heights, says that "the sounds of police sirens is very triggering for [me] because I have PTSD from the war."[62] For residents like Ayaan, the militarized police forces that roamed the streets of City Heights created anxiety. In their eyes, the San Diego police operate like an occupying military force that treats the residents as enemy combatants rather than as people worthy of protection.

The SDPD certainly reminds Barsanji of a military force. "Man!" he says. "You should have seen the police back then. They were like an army, and we were the enemies. The kind of gear the SWAT teams had, it looked like they were ready for war." Nevertheless, Somali refugees would not remain passive victims of police violence; in fact, many Somalis actively developed strategies to help each other survive militarized policing. Barsanji states, "We would help people in the community who had their doors and windows broken by SWAT teams—many people in the community came together to help out these people."[63] Somali refugees resided in close-knit neighborhoods, which enabled them to develop resources to help other refugee families facing police violence. In this context, the "refugee repertoire" functions as a form of community building and counter-policing that mobilizes the limited resources available to Somali refugees in response to governments that are unwilling to adequately provide for them. The refugee repertoire emerged out of the multifaceted forms of state violence that refugees encountered during their harrowing journey that crisscrossed continents. In San Diego, Somali youths deploy the refugee repertoire to navigate racial profiling.

Like many Black people, Somali youths regularly experience racial profiling at the hands of the police. Liban, a young Somali man, shares a story about his intimate experience with racial profiling. "I never sold drugs in my entire life, but I was arrested and charged twice for drug distribution charges. The police with patrol cars would follow me and say we are going to get you and catch you slipping. I was Black, so to them I looked like a drug dealer. I vowed to tell my friends about this officer so they didn't have to experience this."[64] Somali refugees did not passively accept the criminalization of their bodies; rather, Somali youths congregated to discuss methods for navigating police surveillance. Ahmed is a college student who has lived in San Diego since 1999, when he arrived in City Heights as a refugee. He reminisces about his time as a youth in City Heights: "We would help each other out; we would give tips about which places to go to buy things with food stamps like clothes, TVs, and who to trust with food stamps—some stores didn't accept food stamps." Somali youths mobilized what little resources they had to help each other to survive state violence.

Ahmed divulges that the SDPD would regularly force Somali youths to undergo invasive body searches. "Some friends of mine would always get pulled over by the City Heights Library," he says, "and the police would push us against the wall and search our pockets while telling us that we wouldn't amount to shit. Sometimes they would slam our heads against the wall and there is nothing we can do about it."[65] Although Ahmed's experience illustrates the sense of powerlessness Somali refugees feel in the face of police abuse, young Somali activists have sought to overcome this sense of helplessness through collective action guided by their shared experiences and culture. Zach, a Somali activist in the BLM movement, shares how "Somali Americans . . . have been able to really use the Somali language as a tool."[66] The Somali language thus becomes a means for Somali refugees to share information without the fear of police surveillance. It was within these collectives that Somali youth found strength to challenge police violence. These collective projects also functioned as information hubs where Somali youth shared information and resources with each other.

As Somali youths develop solidarity for survival, the police have become increasingly militarized and aggressive. Ahmed's violent encounter with police shows that militarized police forces are far more likely to be aggressive because they are trained to use violence as a first resort. For Black youths, there is a very real danger that encounters with the police will invariably lead to death. A Somali refugee by the name of Ali recalls, "We had to avoid police back then [in 1994]. They walked around the streets of City Heights with armored cars and assault rifles. We warned each other if we knew the police were going to do a raid that day." Hardly passive subjects of militarized violence, Somali refugee youths invented increasingly intuitive strategies to navigate police violence. Ali's story draws on the long history of Somali resistance to state violence. Ali explains, "In Somalia we did the same thing: we warned each other when we knew a rebel group was coming to our village, so people had enough time to leave."[67] Ali's story reveals how Somali refugees utilized community building and knowledge sharing as central strategies for surviving the war, the refugee camps, and militarized policing in the inner city. Therefore, the Somali refugee experience is marked not only by layered forms of state violence but also by resistance to this violence through the development of life-sustaining practices in response to the carceral militarism of state agents and institutions.

The police surveillance that Somali youths encounter in San Diego illuminates the reach and scale of the surveillance state. The state agents who surveil Somali refugees include such disparate actors as teachers, police, social workers, and refugee resettlement workers. These state and nonstate actors increasingly partner with police as part of the push to implement community policing within departments. Community policing programs underscore the ways in which various nonstate agencies work on behalf of the state. Moreover, community policing reveals the myriad ways Somali refugees are policed for their cultural and religious practices, clothing, and reliance on government programs. Somali refugees in the United States are often accused of welfare fraud and, as one news article—titled "Is Welfare Fraud Funding Al-Shabaab?"—argues, of exploiting the welfare system to fund terrorist organizations.[68]

Racial profiling during traffic stops is a common practice. The SDPD criminalizes Black communities by disproportionally issuing tickets to Black people. According to a report by the ACLU of San Diego:

> Among racial and ethnic groups, San Diego Police stopped black people and Pacific Islanders at the highest rates per population. Pacific Islanders were stopped by San Diego police at 126% higher rate per population than white people. Black people were stopped at the highest rates of any other group—a rate 219% higher per population than white people. Black people were more likely to be stopped by police for both traffic violations and also for pedestrian stops.[69]

This ACLU report underscores the heightened levels of surveillance that Black people experience in San Diego. Abdikareem, a Somali refugee who has lived in City Heights for nearly two decades, shares a story that exemplifies the myriad ways that Black people are punished by the carceral state. "I couldn't pay the $250 speeding ticket because I had to choose between paying rent or the ticket, and I chose rent, and afterward, I started getting fees. I eventually spent time in the county jail because I couldn't afford to pay any of it."[70] Abdikareem's story is an example of the criminalization of poverty, which adversely impacts the finances of working-class Black communities. Police routinely target Black motorists for tickets, as well.[71] Black motorists are far more likely to be issued citations than white motorists, so Black people bear the brunt of the financial costs associated with police tickets.

Black people make up 5 percent of San Diego's population yet account for 12 percent of vehicle stops, whereas white people comprise 47 percent of San Diego's population yet just 41 percent of vehicle stops. This discrepancy underscores the ways in which white privilege functions, because white people are more likely to escape police surveillance relative to their demographic representation. The higher rate at which Black San Diegans are stopped by the police means the SDPD is racially profiling Black motorists.

Abdikareem's story reveals the deep racial disparities in policing and the entrenched nature of racial profiling within policing practices. In this statement he captures his sentiments about the stark racial divide in how Black people experience policing in contrast to white people's experience with policing: "I can't tell you how often I get pulled over by the police; it feels like I live in a different world, my world where police are terrifying and the white world where police are the good guys."[72] It is as though Black and white people occupy different worlds.

Abdikareem's visceral experiences with racial profiling are an indictment of these two Americas. Despite the disparity and the heightened levels of police surveillance, Black people are not passive in the face of racial profiling. Abdikareem received money from other Somali refugees to help pay the traffic ticket. He says that in the refugee camps Somali refugees collectively pooled money in a *diya* (a Somali payment group). In the Dadaab refugee camp, Somali refugees would call upon the collective resources of the *diya* to help families that were experiencing hardship. Somali refugees transported this practice to City Heights, San Diego: the refugee repertoire travels across space and time.

Technologies and Counter-Technologies of Policing

A Somali refugee activist who has spent many years advocating for the Somali refugee community in San Diego, Faysal, explains how police utilized surveillance technology to monitor Black youths: "The police in the 1990s had these gang databases that include every Somali teen in San Diego. For many of us, we were in the database because we knew a friend of a friend who was a gang member. The police would come to us every day and say, 'We know you are a gang member; come with us for questioning.'"[73] In this story Faysal is referencing the CalGang database, which has gained notoriety in the past decade. The California State Department of Justice created the CalGang database to track known gang members and their affiliates. Currently the personal information of 150,000 people is stored there. A 2019 report attorney-general report on CalGang revealed the racial demographics of the database and showed that Latinx people represented 64 percent of the people included.[74] In San Diego County, Black people represent 5 percent of the county's population yet are 19 percent of the people in the CalGang database, whereas white people make up 45 percent of the county yet are only 3 percent of people added to the CalGang database.[75] This stunning data reveals a racial disparity in the CalGang database and highlights the fact that Black people are uniformly targeted and tracked by police.

In San Diego, Black youths have had their personal information stored in the CalGang database without their consent and without being informed.[76] The CalGang database has been criticized by the ACLU for its secrecy and violations of civil liberties. There is very little transparency with the CalGang database since the database does not disclose the names of people whose information they possess. In 2013, California Senate Bill No. 458 required law enforcement to notify minors and their guardians if they were listed as known gang members in the database.[77] Even with the passage of this bill, most people cannot access the database to see if their names are listed there. Law enforcement databases such as these disproportionately criminalize Black youths for the offense of associating with their friends. Black youths are already targeted, and they are further criminalized when police pull them over and see their names in the database. According to an article by Cody Dulaney, "Once someone is added to the database, the label of active gang membership affects every other interaction with the justice system—from how a prosecutor handles a first-time low-level offense to how an officer interacts with someone during a traffic stop."[78] Some of the Somali youths I interviewed claimed that SDPD officers would ask for their identification and subsequently enter their information into the CalGang database. The police thus utilized carceral technology to surveil and track Somali refugee youths, resulting in their entrapment into the criminal injustice system.

In *Punished: Policing the Lives of Black and Latino Boys*, Victor Rios details the role of police gang databases: "It appeared that the police classified young people as gang members to benefit from the ability to keep track of them and impose harsher restrictions and policing on them."[79] Gang databases function as tools of surveillance that give police access to data on youths of color. Rios reveals that these crime databases produce the conditions of possibility for police violence. Black people who are tracked in the database are more likely to encounter police violence because the police are looking for them specifically, armed with a litany of personal information made possible by this database. Abdirahim, a Somali refugee activist, recounts his jarring experience with the CalGang database: "This cop who I never saw before pulled up next to me and knew my name, where I lived, and named all of my friends. He told me he was watching me; I was so scared I couldn't understand how he knew who I was."[80] The ominous statement "he was watching me" echoes the Black experience of always being surveilled by people who find the presence of Black people threating and disturbing. Simone Browne urges us "to factor in how racism and antiblackness undergird and sustain the intersecting surveillances of our present order."[81]

Cumar, a Somali activist working in the BLM movement, shares his thoughts on surveillance technology:

> People don't really understand how surveillance really works and how just all of these things are interacting with each other, of just how the library can interact with law enforcement and get your data, or just how social media is a way that folks are getting data as well too. Being able to protect people's digital organizing, digital security, and all of that. We've seen just different things that were used to attack folks and make people scared and not talk.[82]

Another tool of surveillance technology employed by the police is crime mapping. The SDPD produced an interactive map of crime that shows, quite literally, how police map crime onto neighborhoods of color.[83] With this interactive map, the user can view live

[94] CONFRONTING ANTI-BLACK RACISM

updates of crimes specified by area code. The most populated crimes on this website are thefts and vandalism. Upon closer inspection, it appears that a large portion of the crimes are concentrated in the City Heights area of San Diego.

The police map crime onto the Black communities in City Heights to justify the concentration of militarized police forces there.[84] As geographers Hawthorne and Lewis argue, "Race is central to the ways in which particular spaces (and, by extension, the bodies that have been 'fixed' to or 'contained' in those spaces) are constructed as empty, passive, immobile, or expendable or as exploitable sites of accumulation."[85] Therefore, City Heights and the Somalis who live there are constructed as sites of violence and crime that can be disciplined by police intervention. The SDPD claims that armored vehicles and SWAT teams are necessary to combat crime levels in City Heights. Crime mapping is an important part of the ideological project of the SDPD because it designates neighborhoods like City Heights as criminal. The SDPD masks the routine racial profiling that Black people experience in San Diego by drawing attention to crime. I juxtapose the police's mapping of crime with an alternative mapping project produced by Somali youths. This mapping project involves Somali youths gathering information regarding the location of patrol cars and circulating this information among their friends. Somali youths map the location of police to evade police surveillance. This youth-led mapping project can be traced to the shared strategies of survival that emerged from the Somali civil war.

Jamal is a college student who has had numerous experiences with racial profiling in San Diego. He says, "You have to avoid the corner of 47th and University. That place, homie, is where police always harass young Black kids."[86] Jamal's countermapping of the police challenges the police's mapping of Black neighborhoods as criminal. The police map the corner of 47th Street and University Avenue in San Diego as a site of criminality, which is contested by Somali youths who contend that this street corner is a site of police brutality. By recasting the terrain, Somali youths actively respond to and develop strategies to resist the police's project of criminalizing their neighborhoods. The disjuncture between these two mapping projects shows that redefining space can be a means of political and social contestation. As Black feminist geographer Katherine McKittrick argues, "Black geographies are deep spaces and poetic landscapes" in which Black people remake space.[87] Omar is a Somali college student who re-mapped Black space:

> One of my friends bought a police scanner so that we would know what the police are up to. Whenever we found out where there would be a lot of police activity, we would text all our friends and tell them to avoid that region. One time there were ten squad cars at the corner of Fairmount and University. I was terrified by all those cops. I told all my friends to avoid that area so we went to another area, Fairmount and College, where all the Black skaters hang.[88]

Omar's strategy shows how technology often associated with state surveillance can also be utilized for resistance. The counternarratives produced by Somali youths challenge the dominant narrative employed by the state that regards Black bodies and the spaces they inhabit as inherently criminal and deviant.

Militarizing Police

The popular use of terms such as "war zones" and "war on drugs" by police forces reveals that the militarization of the police is both a structural and linguistic phenomenon. The militarized language employed by police is partly conditioned by the targeted recruiting of military veterans by police departments. A wide variety of state-funded programs promote the hiring of veterans, and the SDPD in particular incentivizes the hiring of military veterans onto its force.

Kevin Loria provides an investigative report that details the recruitment of military veterans to police forces. He claims that "under the Justice Department's COPS (Community Oriented Policing Services) program, 629 of the 800 police jobs funded for the next three years—all the newly hired officers—must go to veterans who served at least 180 days' active duty since 9/11. This is the first time the 18-year-old COPS program has required cities and counties seeking grants to hire veterans exclusively."[89] The COPS program epitomizes the steady militarization of police forces in cities across the country. Military veterans are often trained to use lethal force as a first and last measure.[90] Some of the veterans hired by the SDPD had been deployed in places like Somalia and Iraq. Eidle, a Somali refugee who has repeatedly experienced racial profiling at the hands of the SDPD, shares a story about a fateful encounter with an officer in 1998: "The police officer pulled up on me near a 7-Eleven and ran out of the car and shoved me against the wall to search my pockets; when I told him why was he doing this to me he told me, 'Shut up, you stupid skinny.'"[91] The word "skinny" is a derogatory term used by US Marines during the military invasion of Somalia in 1993 to refer to Somalis. The Marines' use of the racial epithet "skinny" grows out of a long history of US military use of degrading and dehumanizing terms to refer to non-Western people: "Gook" was used to refer to Vietnamese people during the US war in Vietnam, and "Hajjis" has been used for Iraqi people. The US military has historically utilized language to dehumanize formerly colonized people who become the target of US imperialism. Eidle's story shows the ways in which racialized epithets travel between the military and police.

These racialized discourses move across borders uninhibited in much the same way the US military does. On the other hand, Somali refugees have not remained passive in the face of racist and dehumanizing words like "skinny"; instead, they have developed their own counter-vocabulary to describe the police, intended to defy the police's utilization of racially coded words like "thug" to refer to Black people. Explaining some of the creative terms employed by Somali youths, Eidle says that "whenever police harassed us and called us names, we call them names too, especially in Somalia we would refer to police as 'Dabal Askar,' and they would look confused."[92] The literal translation of "Dabal Askar" from Somali to English is "stupid police." Epitomizing the weapons of the weak, using this phrase was Somali refugees' response to the daily humiliations suffered at the hands of the police. The counter-vocabularies that Somali youths have developed recall the Black Panthers' deployment of the term "pigs" to refer to police in the 1960s and 1970s.

Conclusion

Police murders are not merely spectacles; rather, violence is endemic to modern policing. As a result of this entrenchment, ending police violence will require radical strategies. With the large-scale Black Lives Matter protests erupting all over the nation in 2020, there has been a push to move beyond the politics of reform. The politics of reform claims that civilian oversight committees and the diversification of police forces are the solution to police violence. The politics of abolition, on the other hand, offers a more radical challenge to policing in America. In cities across the nation, activists have urged for the defunding of police and the redistribution of police resources to social programs that aid Black people. An abolition stance argues that police brutality can never be resolved by the American judicial system because it is the same system that legitimizes and grants police their power to use deadly force. Police abolition offers greater potential for radical change because it imagines a world without police, thereby addressing the structural racism that informs it as an institution.

Moreover, Somali refugees' encounters with militarized policing have increasingly been impacted by the War on Terror. The Somali refugee experience shows how militarized violence abroad influences local policing practices in the United States. This has become more evident with the emergence of counterterrorism task forces within police departments. The War on Terror provided the justification for arming local police with military-grade weapons and equipment. As an article in the *Atlantic* highlights, "Undoubtedly, American police departments have substantially increased their use of military-grade equipment and weaponry to perform their counterterrorism duties, adopting everything from body armor to, in some cases, attack helicopters."[93] Somali refugees, as part of a Black and Muslim community, have experienced the militarization of the police, fueled by the War on Drugs and subsequent criminalization of Blackness and by the War on Terror and criminalization of Muslims. Somali refugees reveal how the War on Drugs and the War on Terror are not disconnected wars but rather related operations crucial to sustaining the US war machine both abroad and domestically.

4 Somali Refugees and the War on Terror

Terrorism Studies

As Black Muslims, Somali refugees have had lived experiences with state violence that illuminate the intersections between Islamophobia and anti-Blackness. A Somali refugee epistemology is rooted in the recognition that different sectors of state power—the FBI, the military, and the police—can be motivated by both Islamophobia and anti-Blackness. State instruments of violence converged, for example, in the 2004 case of Abdullah Jama Amir, a Somali man in City Heights, San Diego, who was first arrested by the San Diego Police Department (SDPD), then detained by ICE, and then sent to Guantanamo Bay by the US military.[1] Amir's case exemplifies the links between anti-Black and anti-Muslim discourses and their impacts on the lived experiences of Somali refugees. In the post-9/11 era, Muslims are imagined to be threats to US interests. The convergence of anti-Black racism and Islamophobia in particular means that the Somali refugee is constructed as a dangerous subject—a criminal and a terrorist—who needs to be eliminated rather than reformed by the state.

This chapter highlights the convergence of Islamophobia and anti-Black racism as a legitimizing apparatus for the mobilization of the military and militarized police against Somali refugees. Police training manuals are juxtaposed with news reports, and Somali counternarratives are juxtaposed with state discourses. The claim is not that anti-Blackness and Islamophobia operate the same way—since Islamophobia and anti-Blackness have different histories and operate in structurally differing ways—but that Somalis who are Muslim and racialized as Black in the United States are impacted and interpellated by both Islamophobia and anti-Blackness.

Scholars have only recently started to examine the intersections between the War on Terror and the War on Drugs, but Somalis have always, often viscerally, felt these connections. Axlam, a Somali refugee residing in City Heights, illustrates the cumulative and violent impact of the War on Drugs and the War on Terror on the Somali refugee community: "When we first came to San Diego in 1993, the police were always attacking us because we are Black and arresting Somalis for no reason. Now, the police harass us because we are Muslim. They attack our families in Somalia; my brother in Somalia tells me he hears American bombs dropped in Mogadishu every night."[2] Axlam immediately makes the connection between domestic US warfare against Black communities in San Diego and foreign warfare against Muslims abroad. This form of knowing is a Somali refugee epistemology that has always understood and felt the scope and reach of US state violence. While Somali refugee youth activists are at the forefront of exposing US counterterrorism programs, state and federal agencies utilize scholarship from the field of terrorism studies to justify surveillance against Somalis. Therefore, I juxtapose the epistemology produced by Somali refugee activists with the one produced by state actors, agencies, and institutions.

The field of terrorism studies produced scholarship that has aided the FBI and police in crafting their counterterrorism programs that equate Muslims with terrorism. In contrast to scholars in the field of terrorism studies, Somali refugee youths produce counternarratives that expose Islamophobia and state violence directed at Muslims. As Faysal Said, a young Somali refugee, eloquently states, "They want to make us seem like terrorists, but the state is the real terrorist."[3] The sharp divergences between the epistemology produced by terrorism studies scholars and the epistemology generated by Somali youth activists come into full view when the work of academic Joseph Clark, who has been at the forefront of the field, is examined closely.

In a 2012 police document titled "Running a Three-Legged Race: The San Diego Police Department, the Intelligence Community, and Counter-Terrorism," Andrew Mills and Joseph Clark argue that the SDPD has a need to establish a counterterrorism unit. They argue that Al-Shabaab, a Somalia-based terrorist organization that took control of parts of the country in 2006, has "emerged as one of the most significant domains identified by the SDPD's new threat picture. San Diego is home to a large Somali population and is a primary point of entry for Somalis claiming asylum. . . . [The Criminal Intelligence Unit's] work to establish intelligence priorities and a collection plan to meet this domain began with the writing of a thorough report about what was known about the local diaspora."[4] Al-Shabaab has been the premier target of US counterterrorism in Somalia. The SDPD invokes the specter of Al-Shabaab to justify its surveillance of the Somali refugee community under the banner of domestic counterterrorism. The SDPD's engagement with counterterrorism highlights how Islamophobic discourses are mobilized by the state to buttress carceral militarism, thereby militarizing the police. Mills and Clark's document reveals that the Somali refugee community has increasingly become a priority target for US counterterrorism in San Diego. The SDPD profiles Somalis as terrorist threats by linking the Somali community in San Diego to Al-Shabaab in Somalia. Mills and Clark posit that Somali youths in San Diego are recruited by Al-Shabaab and therefore constitute a threat to US national security. To counteract this framework, Somali refugee activists like Aamiina, an organizer for Black Lives Matter (BLM), argue, "In our view the police are the terrorist; they terrorize Somali refugees with random stops and police harassment."[5] In contrast to Aamiina's framework, Mills and Clark claim that the Somali refugee community needs to be surveilled by the police to disrupt the radicalization of Somali youths. They encourage the SDPD to collect data about Somali refugees. Clark's role as a coauthor highlights the work academics do toward legitimizing state surveillance.

The paper was published by the Homeland Security Policy Institute, a partnership between George Washington University and the Department of Homeland Security. Digging into the intimate relationship between the state and academia that, among other things, produces Islamophobic discourse, Henry Giroux reveals that the Department of Homeland Security "handles a $70 million scholarship and research budget, and its initiatives, in alliance with those of the military and intelligence agencies, point toward a whole new network of campus-related programs. [For instance,] the University of Southern California has created the first 'Homeland Security Center of Excellence' with a $12 million grant that brought in multi-disciplinary experts from UC Berkeley,

NYU, and the University of Wisconsin-Madison."[6] The funding the Department of Homeland Security gives to universities is an example of the myriad ways academia can be enlisted to buttress the project of US militarism.

Andrew Mills, the first author on this document, was the commanding officer of the Counterterrorism Unit of the SDPD and is currently chief of police for the Palm Springs Police Department. Second author Joseph Clark is an associate professor in the Department of Political Science at Towson University. The relationship between Mills and Clark is indicative of the partnership between the police and certain criminologists in producing crime as racialized threats. Moreover, this partnership also underscores how the SDPD turns to scholarship about Somalis produced by academics like Clark to guide its policies rather than to Somalis themselves. This disregard for Somali experiences and narratives is legitimated by the belief that the only people qualified to analyze the Somali community are "experts." Therefore, I draw from Somali narratives and stories to challenge the racist ideologies produced by terrorist studies scholars, criminologists, and the state regarding the Somali community.

Terrorism studies scholarship is often taken up by the state as a rationale for the violence the state inflicts on Somalis, as in the case of Mohamed Abdihamid Farah. In August 2015, police arrested two Somali men in San Diego with alleged ties to radical extremism. One of the men arrested was an American citizen named Mohamed Abdihamid Farah. A 2016 court document filed by the US District Court of Minnesota shows that an undercover agent was responsible for his apprehension.[7] Such undercover agents often surveil the Somali refugee communities in Minnesota and San Diego. According to the court document:

> This matter is before the Court on the government's motion for Protective Order Pertaining to Undercover Agent [Doc. No. 422].
>
> Based on the files, record and proceedings herein, and after the Court's *in camera* review of the government's submissions disclosing the true name of the Undercover Agent, and the information concerning any prior cases in which the Undercover Agent testified, the Court hereby orders as follows:
>
> IT IS HEREBY ORDERED that the government shall disclose the true name of the Undercover Agent to defense counsel. Defense counsel shall not disclose the Undercover Agent's true name to the defendants. The government shall also disclose to defense counsel the three cases listed in its submission to the Court in which the Undercover Agent provided testimony.

Even though the undercover agent was critical to the capture of Mohamed Farah, the agent's name was only disclosed to the defense counsel, not the defendants. Secrecy is central to the surveillance apparatus of US counterterrorism, which disproportionately targets Muslims. As Critical Refugee Studies scholar Ma Vang reveals, "The refugee as an artifact of US liberal militarized empire and state governance is also a subject of secrecy whose absence in the archives demonstrates record-keeping as one such form of violence."[8] Vang underscores that the erasure of refugee subjects from state documents and archives shows how secrecy functions to hide the violence the state inflicts on refugee subjects. Refugee stories, on the other hand, expose the violence of American empire and of the secrecy that, by design, surrounds its surveillance and detention of refugee and immigrant populations. Axado Hussein, a Somali refugee living in San Diego, explains how "everything the US government is doing for counterterrorism feels like its secret.

We don't even know all the Somalis who have been killed or disappeared by the US government."[9]

The National Defense Authorization Act of 2012 (NDAA) created the conditions of possibility for the indefinite detention and disappearance of Muslims accused of terrorism. This act gave the US government the power to detain people suspected of terrorism; section 1021 outlines the detention of persons suspected of terrorism, enabling "detention under the law of war without trial until the end of the hostilities authorized by the Authorization for Use of Military Force."[10] Although the NDAA allows the US government to detain an individual without trial until the end of hostilities, this effectively means suspects may be detained without trial indefinitely because the War on Terror has no clearly defined end. As Ifrah Hussein, a Somali refugee youth, states, "I feel like the War on Terror is a war on Somalis, and [that it] will never end unless all Somalis are eliminated or renounce their faith."[11] Ifrah's sentiments are supported by the evidence of extreme surveillance that Somali refugees experience at the hands of the state, as well as by the threat that the state can suspend due process if a person is suspected of terrorism. The post-9/11 world engendered a state that can encroach on the civil liberties of its citizens under the guise of security. The FBI and SDPD utilized Mohamed Farah's case to mobilize fears against Muslims in San Diego.

On Being Black and Muslim

While Somali refugees are hyper-visible in state counterterrorism programs, Somalis are often rendered invisible in Muslim organizing spaces. Black Muslims are often erased from narratives around Muslim identity even though they account for one-fifth of the

Muslim population in America.[12] As Khalif Mohamed, a Somali refugee college student in San Diego, explains: "I am Black and Muslim, but in Muslim spaces like mosques and Muslim conventions, other Muslims constantly question my Muslim identity and assume I must be a recent convert because I am Black."[13]

Muslims are generally represented as Arab within the US cultural imaginary. Su'ad Abdul Khabeer, an ethnographer and Muslim studies scholar, argues:

> Muslims have a long history in the United States, beginning with the involuntary migration of enslaved African Muslims. So it is important to note that the rise of the ethnoreligious hegemony of Immigrant Islam is tied to the arrival of a particular cohort of émigrés: Muslims from the Middle East and South Asia who arrived in the United States in larger numbers after the loosening of racialized immigration quotas in 1965. Rather, in the mid-twentieth century US Black American Muslims were the prototypical Muslims on the domestic front.[14]

Abdul Khabeer's analysis highlights how most Black Muslims in America have historically been represented as African American followers of the Nation of Islam. With the arrival of African Muslim migrants in the 1980s and 1990s, the Black Muslim population has become increasingly diverse, with a visible presence of African Muslims in many US cities. Yet despite this heterogeneity of Muslims in America, Muslims and Arabs are viewed as interchangeable—a narrative challenged by the ethnic and religious diversity within Arab communities and the racial diversity within Muslim communities around the world. Therefore, the dominant representation of Arab Muslims in the media as the only legible form of Muslim identity has led to the erasure of African Muslims from popular culture.

According to a Pew Research Center report, "Muslim Americans are racially diverse. No single racial or ethnic group makes up more than 30% of the total. Overall, 30% describe themselves as White, 23% as Black, 21% as Asian, 6% as Hispanic and 19% as other or mixed race."[15] In light of this racial diversity in the Muslim community in America, the discourse of Islamophobia continues to construct Muslims as monolithically Arab and homogenous.

The case of a Somali man by the name of Mustafa Mattan illustrates the erasure of Black Muslims from conversations around Islamophobia and its impacts on Muslim communities in North America. Mattan was shot in his home in Fort Murkararry, Canada, in what many Somali activists describe as a hate crime.[16] In a report on Mustafa's death on Al Jazeera, Khaled Beydoun and Margari Hill argue that "the curious case of Mustafa Mattan is as much a story of intra-racial division and anti-Black racism within the Muslim population as it is a narrative about the neglected death of a young man seeking a better life far from home."[17] The scant media coverage regarding Mattan's murder emphasized his Muslim identity while neglecting to mention his Blackness. Because Blackness and Muslimness are unable to occupy the same position in the US or Canadian cultural imaginary, his Blackness was erased. Mohamed Gedi, a young Somali refugee, eloquently captures this sentiment, "People find it hard to believe that Somalis can be both Black and Muslim; we are never seen as truly Black or Muslim."[18]

Black Muslims have largely been written out of the narratives of the BLM movement, which has focused predominantly on African American men killed by the police. I analyze the case of Abdi Mohamed to shed light on the institutional racism that Black

Muslims experience. In 2016, police shot Somali teen Abdi Mohamed in Salt Lake City, Utah. This police shooting garnered little public attention outside of the Somali community.[19] In response to this erasure, young Somalis initiated a Twitter campaign to bring to light the violence that Black Muslim youths experience at the hands of the police. Somali BLM organizer Sahal stated, "If all Black lives matter, then the lives of Black refugees, immigrants, and Muslims also need to matter."[20] Young Somali activists organized on social media to draw attention to the unique challenges and structural violence that Black Muslims encounter in the United States. These young Somali refugee activists adopted the hashtag #BlackMuslimLivesMatter to highlight the erasure of Black Muslims from discussions around state violence against Black people in America.

Somalis' intersecting identities as Black, Muslim, and refugee link the seemingly disconnected issues of immigrant detention, police brutality, and the War on Terror. Somali refugees are also subjected to the structural violence made possible by the War on Drugs, the War on Terror, and the antiimmigrant policies of the state. Yasmin, a young Somali activist in San Diego, argues:

> We are always left out of conversations regarding immigrants and immigrant justice. People also assume that Black immigrants do not exist, so we have had to organize within immigrant rights groups while also being erased from those spaces. Somalis are also left out of conversations around Islamophobia because some people find it hard to believe that there are Black Muslims or even Black Arabs. Also, we are erased from the Black Lives Matter movement because some people don't see us as Black because we are Muslim and speak a different language.[21]

Yasmin here references the compounding issues affecting Somali refugees that involve immigration being framed as an issue that only affects Asian and Latinx migrants, leaving little room for the structural issues affecting Black immigrants. Therefore, Yasmin is advocating for an intersectional analysis of Islamophobia and immigration that accounts for the ways in which Somali refugees are rendered mute in both Muslim and migrant spaces. Yet Somali activists like Yasmin have worked diligently to make Somali voices heard around issues of counterterrorism and state violence directed at Muslims.

As Yasmin's story highlights, Somali refugees in San Diego are subjected to intense scrutiny by the counterterrorism unit of the SDPD due to Islamophobia. The San Diego Joint Terrorism Task Force (JTTF) is tasked with gathering intel on the Somali refugee community to curtail the radicalization of Muslims in San Diego before it reaches the last stage: "violent action." In 2011, terrorism studies expert Randy Borum produced a chart based on Fathali Moghaddam's "staircase" model of the stages of radicalization, which has influenced the way the FBI and SDPD's JTTF approaches counterterrorism. Borum's chart circulated in various FBI counterterrorism training programs.

Borum's role in developing this chart is indicative of the relationship between the production of racial knowledge and state violence. In an article titled "Radicalization into Violent Extremism," Borum reviews several models of the process of Muslim radicalization. Moghaddam's model encompasses six progressive floors, or stages. Borum claims that the first floor, referred to as "Perceived Options to Unfair Treatment," is the most crucial stage for the purposes of intervention. The discontent toward the "unfair treatment" that Muslims experience is born out of a clear resentment for the Islamophobia and racism that Muslims routinely encounter in America.[22]

Borum's pathway to "radicalization" mirrors the pathway to social change adopted by social justice activists because both share a desire to combat injustice. According to Borum, "These young men have a strong feeling that Muslims are being discriminated against. They observe things that they consider to be unjust. This can be anything from a brother who is hassled by the police or the current events in Iraq or Palestine."[23] Borum cites a study on Muslim youths in Amsterdam to posit that a need for justice is a pathway to radicalization.[24] Therefore, by inference, social justice activists are on the same pathway to radicalization as terrorists. For terrorism studies scholars like Borum, the problem is not racial discrimination but rather the ways in which Muslim youths respond to racial discrimination.

Policing Terrorism

When the Department of Justice manual *Policing Terrorism* was distributed to police departments, it signaled the emergence of counterterrorism in local law enforcement. Ronald Clarke and Graime Newman are the primary authors of this manual. In the manual, subtitled "An Executive's Guide," Newman and Clarke address police chiefs directly: "After the initial shock of 9/11, you, like many other chiefs, might have begun gloomily to contemplate the future of policing. At a stroke, terrorism had replaced crime as the greatest threat to the nation's social order and intelligence agencies had become society's principal guardians, usurping the role traditionally held by police."[25] Clarke's articulation of social order is premised on the protection of private property, which is a foundational to Western liberalism. The SDPD has taken up the rhetoric of maintaining the social order to assert the need for more police resources dedicated to counterterrorism. The SDPD maintains the need to put more police resources toward counterterrorism by racializing Somali refugees as a threat to the social order in San Diego. The conception of social order is premised on the demonization of Black people as inherent threats to social order and to whiteness broadly.

In 2009, the SDPD created a counterterrorism division tasked specifically with surveilling the Somali refugee community.[26] This newly formed unit was housed within the SDPD's intelligence unit. According to the San Diego County Sheriff's Department, the Terrorist Early Warning Unit or TEW is "a multi-agency task force focused on terrorism-specific intelligence and information-sharing. Participating agencies include the San Diego Sheriff's Department, Federal Bureau of Investigation (FBI), California Department of Justice, California Highway Patrol, Federal Department of Homeland Security (DHS), and Governor's Office of Homeland Security."[27]

The SDPD's interest in Somalis as domestic terrorist threats is striking in light of the fact that Somali refugees represent a relatively small part of San Diego's population. According to the Somali Family Service, as of 2020, the Somali refugee community numbered 30,000 out of a total San Diego population of 1.3 million.[28] Despite the small numbers and the scarcity of Black people in San Diego, Somalis continue to be hyper-visible targets of the police. Somalis are a Black Muslim group whose identities as Black and Muslim are marked as inherently suspect by the SDPD's deployment of the discourses both of Black criminality and of

[112] SOMALI REFUGEES AND THE WAR ON TERROR

Islamophobia. The Blackness of Somali refugees renders them vulnerable to surveillance "technologies of seeing that sought to render the (Black) subject outside of the category of the human."[29] Surveillance technologies directed at Somali refugees, like undercover agents entering Somali mosques, are ways of seeing that link the Black body as always already criminal.

The use of undercover agents is an example of how the state also actively utilizes strategies from the War on Drugs in pursuing its counterterrorism program. Another connection between the War on Drugs and the War on Terror is the so-called comprehensive gang model. The comprehensive gang model is a policing strategy premised on the idea that police departments must partner with local communities to deter gang recruitment.[30] This model was initially developed for drug enforcement but was later adopted by the SDPD as part of its counterterrorism strategy. The Department of Justice provides the following brief overview of the comprehensive gang model: "formal and informal social control procedures, including close supervision or monitoring of gang youth by agencies of the criminal justice system and also by community-based agencies, schools, and grassroots groups."[31] Adopting this gang model as an integral component of its counterterrorism program, the SDPD asks the Somali community to be actively involved in monitoring and surveilling their friends and neighbors for the project of counterterrorism. As a result, the apparatuses of state violence are no longer external, but rather the community becomes an extension of the mechanisms of state surveillance.

A public records request made by the Somali Women's Advocacy Group in conjunction with the ACLU San Diego discovered the impact of this surveillance on the Somali refugee community:

Based on complaints that law enforcement engages in continual surveillance and invasive searches of Somalis in San Diego, the San Diego ACLU called on the FBI and San Diego Police Department to turn over all records related to investigations of the Somali community in San Diego. A sampling of the incidents include: a recent FBI raid in which agents conducted extensive home searches and seized personal documents and computers; agents asking residents which "tribe" they were from, while indicating they already knew the answer; Somali women publicly humiliated by being forced to sit outside without any head coverings and in their night clothes; dozens of FBI agents carrying automatic weapons into a home, terrorizing the small children who witnessed the raid.[32]

The image of FBI agents carrying automatic weapons and inflicting terror on the Somali children who witnessed the raid challenges the law enforcement framework that casts Somalis as terrorist threats by highlighting state violence directed at Somalis. Moreover, the ACLU and the Somali Women's Advocacy group reveal that the Somali refugee community in San Diego fled state violence in Somalia only to encounter it yet again in America.

The JTTF's use of government informants creates paranoia within the Somali community. During my interviews, numerous participants relayed to me their anger that the JTTF was wiretapping their phones. Caaisho, a local Somali refugee in San Diego, says: "I know the FBI is listening to our conversations. It just upsets me to know that I can't get any privacy because I am Muslim. I try to talk in Somali, but I am pretty sure the FBI has a Somali translator working for them. It is crazy to think I am denied my civil liberties simply for being Muslim."[33] Her relative certainty that "the FBI has a Somali translator working for them" is supported under section 205 of the Patriot Act, which allows for the "employment of translators" by the FBI.[34] Hiring Somali translators heightens the levels of surveillance that Somali communities experience. Somali refugees have the legitimate fear that the FBI is listening to their conversations and that speaking the Somali language no longer provides a means to avoid detection and surveillance. Moreover, Caiisho's statement underscores the multitude of ways that Somalis struggle to resist state surveillance. The understandable fear and paranoia caused by government surveillance has led Somali families to refrain from discussing political topics over the phone. The War on Terror and the Patriot Act has increased the state's power to surveil its citizens.

Police officers working on the JTTF are legally recognized as both state and federal law enforcement agents. According to the SDPD's website, the JTTF is "a Federal Bureau of Investigations-based and operated task force. This task force is responsible for conducting assessments, investigations and field interviews of potential and known terrorist threats within the San Diego region. Officers assigned to this task force are also cross-sworn as federal officers."[35] Counterterrorism programs grant police officers federal powers, thereby blurring the line between federal and state law enforcement. The JTTF includes among its members the FBI, military officers, and local police, who all work so closely together that they are essentially entangled. The emergence of counterterrorism within police has also made policing more transnational in scope, and the expansion of policing beyond state and national boundaries signals police departments' increasing global reach.

According to an ACLU report on the militarization of the police, "Using these federal funds, state and local law enforcement agencies have amassed military arsenals purportedly to wage the failed War on Drugs, the battlegrounds of which have disproportionately been in communities of color."[36] The War on Drugs and the War on Terror have no definite end because the state continues to deploy moral panics around Black criminality and Muslim terrorism to legitimatize the targeting of these communities for surveillance and racial profiling.

In "Running a Three-Legged Race," Mills and Clark explain the specific challenges of profiling suspects in counterterrorism policing:

> The homegrown jihadists that threaten the US are not easily identifiable on the basis of demographic characteristics. Today's threat is not borne by the stereotypically thick-accented angry young Arab of a Hollywood film. Of the cases for which ethnicity could be determined, only a quarter are of Arab descent, while 10% are African-American, 13% are Caucasian, 18% are South Asian, 20% are of Somali descent, and the rest are either mixed race or of other ethnicities.[37]

The work of Mills and Clark was critical to the establishment of the counterterrorism task force in San Diego and to the development of its tactics. Mills and Clark claim that 20 percent of all homegrown terrorists are of Somali descent, even though Somali refugees represent 0.02 percent of San Diego's total population.[38] Mills and Clark's assertion that "homegrown militants do not fit any . . . profile" is designed to enable the government to rebuff criticism of racial profiling while employing tactics that specifically target Somali refugees. In this way, the Somali community's Muslimness served as a new basis for casting them as a racialized threat that justified the extraordinary powers granted to the SDPD in their new remit to counter domestic counterterrorism. Moreover, as Somali refugee youth Abdiraxman Sayid says, "The joint terrorist task force is the real threat to the Somali refugee community, but they portray Somalis as threats and terrorists in hiding."[39]

In *Policing the Crises*, Stuart Hall et al. theorizes how police mobilize racial crises to justify the surveillance directed at Black communities.[40] With regard to the Somali community in San Diego, the SDPD have sought public support by using the same language of racial crises to create a moral panic around terrorism. In the quote above, Mills and Clark employ this discourse more subtly, exploiting the fear of a secretive Muslim enemy—one who can hide among the American population—to rationalize the SDPD's extended powers of profiling, surveillance, and detention over Somalis in San Diego. The police are thus able to marshal resources, including military equipment, with public support because the discourse of terror has produced a permanent state of fear. This is the same discourse of terror that helps the US military galvanize resources and expand its global reach.

The US military operates under a permanent state of war by instrumentalizing the fear of the Muslim other. This permanent state of war is occasionally interrupted by shifting geographies of terror. This shifting geography is best highlighted by former president Barack Obama's policy of withdrawing troops from Iraq while also sending twenty thousand soldiers to Afghanistan. As a complex set of intersecting ideas and policies, the War on Terror grants legitimacy to the state's ability to effectively target with military force any country it deems a terrorist threat. The shifting geographies of US military terror have allowed the state to commit more forces to Somalia, which is now recognized as a new front in the War on Terror.

The War on Terror and domestic counterterrorism have disproportionately impacted Muslim communities in the United States. Hashim, a Somali college student in San Diego, has experienced the terror the state inflicts on Somali Americans. Hashim says, "I hate flying because the last time I flew to Somalia to visit my grandmother, I was detained for forty-eight hours by the FBI at the San Diego airport. They said I was from Al-Shabaab."[41] Hashim's story underscores the interconnected nature between the violence Somali people experience in San Diego and Somalia. Hashim's lived experience reveals the naturalization of violence against Muslims and the institutionalization of this violence within the US criminal justice system.

Constructing her own counternarrative, a City Heights resident and Somali refugee named Bishaaro says, "White men with long beards who want to convert to Islam come to spy on us in Somali restaurants, safari market, and in our neighborhoods, but we know who they really are."[42] The men Bishaaro refers to are most likely undercover agents from the counterterrorism unit of the SDPD. The counterterrorism unit, trained by the FBI on surveillance techniques, sends white agents to spy on the Somali community. These agents have long beards and claim to be new converts to Islam to gain access to the Somali community, but Somalis easily see through these attempts to fit the profile of the white Islamic convert. Bishaaro's retort—"we know who they really are"—calls upon a refugee epistemology that makes visible seemingly invisible manifestations of state power. I became aware of the activities of the SDPD's counterterrorism unit because of my interviews with the Somali refugee community in San Diego. The SDPD justifies surveilling the Somali community by claiming that San Diego is a terrorist hotspot because of the large presence of Muslim immigrants and the proximity to the US-Mexico border.

An FBI training manual on Islam, titled "Islam 101," which was distributed to the SDPD in 2011, directly correlates violence with the religion.[43] Figure 1, reproduced from this manual, attempts to quantify the degree of violence and militancy between the ideologies of the Quran, the Bible, and the Torah. On the *y* axis is a range that moves from violent to nonviolent, whereas on the *x* axis is the passage of time from 1400 BCE to 2010 CE. We learn that both the Torah and the Bible started as scriptures that espoused violence and steadily became less violent over time. On the other hand, adherents to the Quran have apparently been espousing violence since its inception, and the level of Islamic violence remains unchanged to the present day. This chart suggests a progressive, linear temporality, which posits that societies become more advanced over time, moving from savagery to modernity. In this linear narrative, the nations of the Christian West are the measuring sticks against which all other cultures are judged as deficient, backward, or "underdeveloped." Just as the discourse of linear progress privileges the "developed" West over the "developing" global south so, too, in cultural terms, Muslim-majority societies are viewed as having remained stuck in time, unchanged since 610. As an African nation and a predominantly Muslim nation, Somalia is doubly cast as a society stuck in the past and also out of place in the modern world.

The United States tried to destroy Somalia through war while also attempting to develop it through aid and state building. This schizophrenic strategy epitomizes US military policy in Somalia. As Somali experiences with state violence are transnational, the activism of San Diegan Somali youths reveals that Somali resistance to state violence has also been transnational in scope. Bishaaro

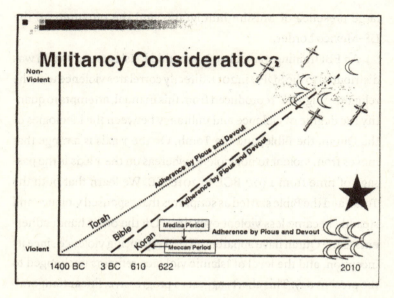

FIGURE 1. FBI diagram visualizing Islamic militancy compared to Judaism and Christianity. Source: Materials from FBI training presentation, originally obtained by *Wired*.

argues, "The US military is killing Somalis in Somalia, and the police are racially profiling and killing Somalis in America."[44]

As Bishaaro knows, US military operations in Somalia are deeply intertwined with the actions of the SDPD because the police and military both mobilize the specter of Al-Shabaab and militant Islam to justify the surveillance of Somalis in San Diego and in Somalia. The FBI's chart on Islamic militancy signals a discursive move that narrates violence as an inherent and unchanging marker of Muslim identity. Thus, the state argues that violence is the only means to suppress Islam broadly and Muslim extremists specifically. This FBI training manual sustains the discourse that undergirds US imperialism because it locates the figure of the

Muslim-as-terrorist as the universal threat to US empire. The War on Terror has also seen the development of new technologies of war and surveillance.

Somali Casualties in the War on Terror

In this section, I investigate the violent repercussions of state surveillance and the many ways state surveillance exposes Somalis to premature death. Citing a 2014 story by Jeremy Scahill in *The Nation*, a Human Rights Watch news report highlights some of the nefarious activities of the military and CIA in Somalia:

> In 2014, *The Nation* reported that CIA agents also regularly interrogated Al Shabab suspects in a basement prison in Somalia and kept Somali intelligence agents there on the agency payroll. The detainees included men illegally handed over to Somalia from neighboring Kenya, including in at least one case based on intelligence provided by the US, the report said. Former detainees told *The Nation* the prisoners were held in filthy, insect-infested, windowless cells, that they were never allowed outdoors, and that some prisoners had been held without charge or trial for months or years.[45]

As this Human Rights Watch report indicates, the violence US militarism enacts on Somalis is hidden from public view and rationalized as necessary for the global War on Terror. The resulting violence these men experience at the hands of the state is part and parcel of the normalization of US military violence. The traumatic violence Muslims experience at the hands of US imperialism is hidden to most, but to the people living in Somalia, it is a quotidian fact of life.

Moreover, secrecy is a critical component of the functioning of US imperialism. Somali activists have been central in exposing the violence of US imperialism. Somali refugee activists make visible the seemingly invisible manifestations of state violence. For Somali refugees, the violence of the state is always already present and visible. Maxamed Farah, a Somali activist, says, "We know that at any point you can be killed by the police or detained by the FBI, and no one would know but your family."[46] The comment "no one would know but your family" references a form of knowing and seeing rooted in the experiential knowledge of Somali refugees, which I name the Somali refugee epistemology. While the violence of the state is visible to Somalis, the state continues to camouflage the surveillance directed at Somali refugees.

Therefore, the ways in which state violence against Muslims is rendered mute is in stark contrast to the hyper-visible representations of the figure of the Muslim terrorist in the media and popular culture. Thus the ways that Muslims are rendered visible and invisible in the media work together to mask US imperial violence and accentuate Islamophobia. A neoconservative think tank produced a film that exemplifies this hyper-visibility of the Muslim terrorist in public discourse: *The Third Jihad: Radical Islam's Vision for America*.[47] *The Third Jihad* is a film that does the work of legitimizing US imperialism by portraying Muslims as threats to the United States and its citizens. The film uses a documentary-style approach to lend a reality effect to the (implausible) theme of Muslims taking over the White House, which, in the film, is carried out by Muslim American citizens. A *New York Times* article by Michael Powell describes the film's distribution to the New York Police Department as a training exercise to prepare its officers to combat domestic terrorism:

Ominous music plays as images appear on the screen: Muslim terrorists shoot Christians in the head, car bombs explode, executed children lie covered by sheets and a doctored photograph shows an Islamic flag flying over the White House. "This is the true agenda of much of Islam in America," a narrator intones. "A strategy to infiltrate and dominate America.... This is the war you don't know about." This is the feature-length film titled "The Third Jihad," paid for by a nonprofit group, which was shown to more than a thousand officers as part of training in the New York Police Department.[48]

A central member of the film's cast is the Somali politician Ayaan Hirsi Ali, who happened to be a major spokesperson for Dutch right-wing parties.[49] Ali's entrenched criticism of Islam shows that the state also employs conservative Somalis to justify the violence it enacts on Somalis. Conservative Somalis make broad, authoritative statements regarding Islam and Somali cultural practices specifically in order to grant credibility to their Islamophobic claims. Ali describes herself as a former Muslim and a critic of Islam, which, according to her, is a religion steeped in barbarism and violence.

Ali has championed Islamophobia for decades and is an ardent critic of immigrants as well. As a self-identified former Muslim who espouses the evils of Islam, she continues to be a central figure in cultural discourses that equate Muslims with terrorism. Ali argues that violence is a fundamental doctrine of Islam, and, as a result, she contends that Islam cannot be recuperated as a religion and must be banished in order for civilization to move forward unhindered by its barbarism. In her autobiography, *Infidel*, Ali asserts that "in the past fifty years the Muslim world has been catapulted into modernity. From my grandmother to me is a journey of just two generations, but the reality of that voyage is millennial. Even today you can take a truck across the border into Somalia and find you have gone back thousands of years in time."[50] In this passage Ali deploys the colonial discourse of savagery that locates Somalia on a different temporal plane from the West. According to Ali, modernity is defined by Europe specifically and whiteness broadly, whereas Somalia is trapped in a primordial past. The film introduces Islam as a marker of racial difference by employing Ali's Islamophobic discourses.

The final scene of *The Third Jihad* shows Muslim Americans taking over the country and establishing Sharia law. The message of the film is clear: police are the vanguards of freedom and democracy against the enemy within, "the Muslim." The NYPD stopped using this film as part of its counterterrorism training when journalists exposed the film to the broader public. New York Civil Liberties Union Executive Director John Lieberman released a statement regarding the use of this film: "The attempted cover-up of the scope of the NYPD's involvement in the creation of the film 'The Third Jihad' by the Department's top brass is the latest in a pattern of misinformation and spin by the Department on issues of serious concern to all New Yorkers."[51]

Nonetheless, the damage had been done, as many police officers had already viewed the film and been trained with it. As a cultural object, *The Third Jihad* functions as a discursive tool for US imperialism because it legitimizes the actions of the US military and police: Muslims in this film are portrayed as literal threats to democracy that need to be dealt with using force. Here, Muslims are imminent threats to the values of American liberalism.

Liberalism is a political philosophy organized around the valorization of the individual and a rejection of collective modes of being. Anthony Bogues characterizes the relationship between US imperialism and liberalism as an "'imperial liberalism' [that] can be understood as an empire of liberty'" and "American imperial power as an empire of liberty, an empire in which conceptions of American liberty are the single truth."[52] The proponents of "imperial liberalism" portray Islam as antithetical to this only truth, thereby making Islam the enemy of liberal democracy. In rejecting individualism, the liberal imperialists argue, the followers of Islam must be regarded as a people trapped in premodern modalities of being hostile to and out of sync with the modern world characterized by individual freedom as it has developed in the Christian West:

> For Europe, this meant that migrants from the global South were not only presumed to hail from an earlier time but to remain stuck in it, thus creating European minority populations perceived to be permanently out of place and time. That is, the putative incompatibility of Islam and Europe is not framed as a conflict between a Christian majority and a Muslim minority, both of whom are European, but between a twenty-first-century European society, committed to multicultural values, gender equality, and sexual freedom, on the one hand, and a medieval, intolerant, foreign culture, on the other.[53]

Fatima El-Tayeb here shows how the juxtaposition of Europe, as a space of tolerance and equality, and Islam, which is defined by backwardness and intolerance, allows Europe to claim superiority and disguise its own intolerance by defining itself against Muslims. This claim that Europe is a space of tolerance is clearly contradicted by the institutional racism that Europeans of color experience in many European countries. A similar Islamophobic opposition operates in the United States, where Somalia and Somali refugees are respectively read as incapable of adopting democracy and unwilling to assimilate. The belief that Islam is antithetical to Western liberalism is a guiding principle of much of the intellectual work in the field of terrorism studies. This foundational philosophy within terrorism studies draws from Samuel Huntington's clash of civilizations thesis, which argued that Islam is incommensurable with Western civilization.[54] This clash between Islam and the West has entered a new chapter with the emergence of drone strikes as a lethal tool in the War on Terror.

Drones and the War on Terror

Drone technology traces its history to the British colonial use of bombs as a method of suppressing colonial resistance. According to Mahmood Mamdani, the first "systematic aerial bombings were carried out by the British Royal Air Force against Somalis in 1920."[55] During the British colonial occupation of Somalia, aerial bombs were used against Africans, who were deemed uncivilized by the British and therefore undeserving of empathy. The British empire deemed Somalis as less than human and therefore made no distinction between civilians and enemy combatants on the ground. Similarly, the War on Terror would see not only the global expansion of US military force but also the emergence of drones as a tool of warfare. Drone strikes often ignore the line between civilians and soldiers because they kill indiscriminately. Drones are indicative of what the War on Terror represents for Somalis: a constant vulnerability to faceless, deadly violence at the hands of the state.

The 2019 Amnesty International report *The Hidden US War in Somalia* explains the US military's rationale for the indiscriminate killings in Somalia:

> According to the understanding of General Bolduc [Commander, Special Operations Command Africa]—who directly confirmed the following to Amnesty International—since being designated as an "area of active hostilities," individuals in these areas of Somalia are now considered to be lawfully targetable based solely on four criteria: age, gender, location (i.e., being inside specific areas—areas in which the US military has deemed the population to be supporting or sympathetic to Al-Shabaab), and geographical proximity to Al-Shabaab. "The reason President Trump changed the rules is because now these guys can be hit," General Bolduc said to Amnesty International. "They are in close proximity, they are part of the Al-Shabaab network. They're *there*. When you are looking at a training camp and all you can see are military-aged males, you say, hey, that's a target."[56]

Ever since Somalia was designated as an "area of active hostilities" by Donald Trump, Somalis, regardless of affiliation with Al-Shabaab, are considered targets for drone strikes. Due to faulty intelligence and indiscriminate violence, drones generally create civilian casualties. An Al Jazeera article documents one Somali father's encounter with drones and the devastating horrors they inflict on Somalis, particularly women and children: "They killed my daughter. She is not even well. They injured two of my daughters, one 14 years and another nine years. They also injured my mother who is very old. We are powerless and they know it. Only God can stop them."[57] Despite horrific stories like this, the US government has not compensated the families of Somali civilians killed in drone attacks. As the Amnesty International report points out:

> Amnesty International was unable to find any information to suggest that compensation or even solatia (condolence) payments had been made following any of the air strikes in Somalia in the past two years. In response to a specific query on this from Amnesty International, a [Department of Defense] spokesperson confirmed in March 2019 that the USA had made no solatia or ex-gratia payments in Somalia because "as previously stated, there are no assessed civilian casualties resulting from US military operations."[58]

Drones are utilized against people whose humanity means little to the state; to be racialized as the other is to be denied the privilege of empathy. A description by a former military officer included in Jeremy Scahill's *Dirty Wars* reveals the indiscriminate nature of drone missions:

> We were much more successful using the surgical strikes, where we went in, to tell you the truth very Israeli like—and we did the drone strike, and/or hellfire strike and we blasted the individual car of a known guy who was known to be in that vehicle. We flew in, we snatched his body, we confirmed it, we got the intelligence and went away. That's the way we should be doing it. We could have been doing that for the preceding (ten) years.[59]

This indiscriminate violence against civilians is not surprising because civilian casualties, or what the US military refers to as "collateral damage," have been a key aspect of the War on Terror. Abdirazak Mohamed, a Somali refugee shop owner in San Diego, explains that "the worst part about US drones is that you hear them before you see them, and this creates the most amount of fear."[60] Drones not only instill the fear of indiscriminate violence in Somali people but also produce a sonic terror for those living in areas of Somalia where drones are active.

As a discourse that reduces Muslims to illiberalism and terrorism, Islamophobia dehumanizes Muslims and has been utilized to sanction the deaths of hundreds of thousands of civilians in the wars on Iraq and Afghanistan. Neta C. Crawford's 2018 report, *Human Cost of the Post-9/11 Wars: Lethality and the Need for Transparency*, provides the following data: "The first such [Department of Defense] report was released in June 2018. It reported that in 2017, 499 civilians were killed in Iraq, Syria, Afghanistan and Yemen and 167 civilians were injured in US operations. An additional 450 reports of civilian casualties for that year 'remained to be assessed.'"[61] The US media, on the other hand, often fail to note civilian casualties, lumping them together with combatants under the category of "insurgents." Civilian casualties stemming from the US War on Terror rarely receive media coverage. Rather, to use US miliary terminology, civilian casualties are viewed as "collateral damage." And, as collateral damage, the victims do not have names or personal biographies; they are objects of state violence and are therefore denied individuality and empathy.

The military's use of drones perpetuates the dehumanization of Muslims, as drones are impersonal weapons, operated by pilots far removed from the reality of the human costs of their actions. In an article from 2015, Jack Serle of the Bureau of Instigative

Journalism reported the increased role of drones in US operations in Somalia:

> It was the fifth consecutive strike against al Shabaab's leadership, with drones now appearing to have superseded other, manned aircraft and cruise-missiles in the seven years since attacks began in Somalia.
>
> The unmanned systems are now widely seen as the US's weapon of choice in its war on terror, as they can "strike their targets with astonishing precision," according to CIA director John Brennan.
>
> But despite their vaunted precision, there are reports the latest strike in Somalia, on January 31, killed or injured civilians.[62]

In this news report, the murder of Somali civilians appears as a mere afterthought in an otherwise successful operation—a metric for the success of the American military. In another report, Serle claims that 150 Somalis were killed in a drone attack that took place on March 7, 2016. This attack marked, at the time, the single highest death toll in a US drone attack recorded anywhere.[63] Rather than condemning this extreme form of violence, the US military celebrated these deaths. The discourse of terror reduces the complexity of Somali humanity to numbers on a military death list.

In 2020, the US military finally acknowledged civilian casualties from drone strikes. According to the US Africa Command:

> Regarding the February 23, 2019, strike, we assess that it is likely that two civilians were regrettably and unintentionally killed and three were injured as a result of the airstrike that also killed two al-Shabaab terrorists who were the intended targets.

"While we follow very precise and rigorous standards, in instances where we fail to meet our expectations, we will admit the mistake," said [US Army Gen. Stephen] Townsend. "Regrettably two civilians were killed and three others injured in a February 2019 airstrike. We have the highest respect for our Somali friends and we are deeply sorry this occurred."[64]

Despite acknowledging the deaths of two Somali civilians, the US military has done nothing to compensate the families of these two victims. According to Hawa Hussein, a Somali refugee living in San Diego, "There is no justice for Somalis killed by the US military."[65] Amnesty International claims a further five Somali civilians have been killed by the US military, a number the US military firmly disputes.[66] Somali activists believe the number to be far higher than five: Hawa states "I don't believe the US military's accounting because they refused to acknowledge any civilian casualties for twelve years. I am sure far more Somalis have been killed or injured than we know or can document."[67]

The US military holds that the difference between the US military and Al-Shabaab is that they do not target civilians. According to US Army General Stephen Townsend: "There is no secret air or shadow war as some allege . . . How can there be when the whole world knows we are assisting Somalia in their fight against al-Shabaab terrorists? When we publicly announce every single airstrike we conduct? When we publicly admit to our mistakes? Unlike al-Shabaab we do everything in our power to avoid civilian casualties and that is not changing on my watch."[68] General Townsend claims that the US military does everything in its power to avoid civilian casualties, yet this is contradicted by the narratives of Somalis whose families have been killed in drone strikes. The distinction between Al-Shabaab as a terrorist organization and the terror the US military inflicts on Somalis blurs with every airstrike that kills Somali civilians. Somalis have not found justice from the state, but the truth is exposed through the stories their families share and the activism these stories inspire. As Hawa explains, "It is up to Somalis to let the world know what the US military is doing, just like BLM activists in America exposed police brutality directed at Black people."[69] Therefore, counternarratives like this one run up against the dominant narratives in the news media that portray Somalis as terrorists and violent threats to the state. The news media is one institution that works to legitimize the violence of the US military and mask the murders of Somali civilians by the state.

Stories published in the *San Diego Union-Tribune* trace the evolution of discourses over time, and the newspaper has a long history of publishing racialized articles regarding Somali refugees. The newspaper first began publishing articles about Somalis in the early 1990s, around the same time that the first wave of refugees arrived in San Diego. These original articles centered on the narrative of Somalis as refugees in need of saving. This humanitarian discourse masked the US militarism that produced the Somali refugee crisis in the first place. In the wake of 9/11, the *Union-Tribune* began publishing stories racializing Somalis as terrorists. This type of journalism legitimizes not only the US military presence in Somalia but also the racial profiling of Somalis in San Diego. In 2019, an article appeared in the *Union-Tribune* headlined "US Citizen Raised in San Diego Faces New Terrorism Charges." Elliot Spagat, the author of the article, reported,

"Today, Mostafa is believed to be the highest-ranking United States citizen fighting overseas for a terrorist organization," said Scott Brunner, the agent in charge of the FBI office in San Diego.

The group claimed responsibility for two Sept. 30 attacks on US and European military targets in Somalia, including one by an estimated 25 fighters who were killed when they tried to storm the Belidogle military airstrip, which hosts Somali and US forces.

Mostafa was born in Waukesha, Wisconsin, and raised in San Diego, where authorities say he has relatives. He graduated from the University of California, San Diego, in 2005 and—according to an FBI poster offering a $5 million reward for information leading to his arrest—joined al-Shabaab around 2006.[70]

Here we find the dominant narratives that portray Somalis as terrorist threats and the US military as the force that can quell terrorism.

The *Union-Tribune* focuses on Somali terrorism at the expense of the multifaceted and creative activities of the Somali community and thereby normalizes US militarized violence directed at the Somali community. Somali activists themselves, on the other hand, reveal the terror of US militarism and state violence broadly. Nimo Mohamed, a Somali refugee activist in San Diego, states:

> We are fighting to expose the violence committed by the US military in Somalia and the horrible things the US military does to Muslims across the world. We also believe this violence is linked to the police violence communities of color experience in San Diego. The news media just focuses on depicting Muslims as terrorists and Black people as criminals. It's our job then to challenge the way the media depicts our communities. Just yesterday, ten Somalis were killed by US drone strikes, and no one seemed to care. It is as if Black lives don't matter to the US government.[71]

Nimo links the violence Somalis encounter in Somalia at the hands of the state to the violence Somalis encounter in San Diego. In her comments, she challenges the pathologizing of Somali refugees by spotlighting the role of US imperialism in making Somalis vulnerable to state violence. The SDPD and the *Union-Tribune* together mobilize the specter of Al-Shabaab to spur fears of Muslims and subsequently rationalize the need for a counterterrorism program.

The US military also mobilizes the figure of Al-Shabaab to justify surveilling Somali refugee communities in San Diego and Somalia. The US military utilizes drones to track Al-Shabaab in Somalia. These drones not only visit death on Somalis but also help the state collect intel by taking photographs of Somalis and the landscape. In a 2015 article in *Foreign Policy*, Ty McCormick reported that a secret US military base was responsible for drones that have wreaked havoc on Somali lives. McCormick quotes a source in the Somali government about the presence of drones in Somalia:

> "They have a base over there," Abdighani Abdi Jama, state minister for the presidency in the interim regional administration in Kismayo, said of U.S. forces, gesturing to a heavily fortified compound not far from the airport's small terminal. He confirmed that as many as 40 U.S. military personnel are currently stationed in Kismayo, roughly 300 miles south of the capital of Mogadishu, where he said they operate drones from the airport's single runway and carry out covert "intelligence" and "counterterrorism" operations.[72]

The secrecy with which the US military operates in Somalia is evident in this report. Local Somalis have been at the forefront of exposing this military base and the secret operations carried out by the US military. Abdinasir is a Somali activist in San Diego, and he traveled to Somalia in 2018. Abdinasir says that "when I was in Mogadishu, I would hear drones. A lot of the folks who lived there told me that they knew the US had several secret military bases. Sometimes Somalis would disappear and be taken to these bases to be tortured and jailed. The US military has tried to keep these bases secret, but Somali activists and journalists have worked hard to expose these bases."[73] Abdinasir reveals that Somali activists have been critical agents in exposing the proliferation of secret military bases in Somalia. He highlights the ways in which Somali storytelling functions to expose US military violence and spread community knowledge through stories.

The drones that emerge out of this secret military base provide visual proof of US military operations in Somalia. The US military continues to deny the existence of this military base. The online publication the *Intercept* has unearthed five secret US military bases in Somalia via open records requests. According to the *Intercept*'s Nick Turse:

> Since 9/11, the US military has built a sprawling network of outposts in more than a dozen African countries. *The Intercept* has obtained US military documents and a set of accompanying maps that provide the locations of these African bases in 2019, including the one at Manda Bay. These formerly secret documents, created by the Pentagon's Africa Command and obtained via the Freedom of Information Act, offer an exclusive window into the footprint of American military operations in Africa.[74]

This formerly secret US military document shows that the US military has set up Somalia as the next target for US imperialism. Some of the military bases on this list have never been revealed to the public, while others are official known military bases. This map highlights the expansive presence of the US military in Africa and the encroachment of the US military onto the African continent under the guise of fighting terrorism. According to this map, the five military bases in Somalia are in Baledogle, Bosasso, Galcayo, Kismayo, and Mogadishu—and there may in fact be more military bases in Somalia than those listed. The nefarious operations of these previously secret bases reveal that state power can also operate in the shadows. The secret bases in Somalia allow the state to surveil Somalis while remaining hidden from the scrutiny that would certainly follow the horrors it visits on Somalis.

State power that operates covertly through nonbeing is difficult to contend with. This state power makes itself visible through the violence it enacts on Muslim bodies. Somali youth activists argue that one solution is to expose US military violence. They say that we can challenge US imperialism by shedding light on the atrocities committed by the US government. Caaliyah Hussein, a Somali refugee activist, says that "our job as Somalis is to show to the world the horrible things the US military is doing to our brothers and sisters in Somalia. They cannot keep killing us in secret; we have to organize to show the world what the US military is doing in Somalia."[75] Activists like her disrupt the normalization of state violence by exposing state violence to public scrutiny. The 2019 Amnesty International report *The Hidden US War in Somalia* confirms what so many Somali activists have been saying:

> The first of two strikes missed the apparent target, killing two civilians, and injuring five civilians, including two children, who were residing in the Farah Waeys settlement next to the road at the time

of the attack. The second strike destroyed the vehicle and killed the suspected Al-Shabaab fighters inside. On 6 December 2017, five civilians, including two children, were killed when a truck carrying suspected Al-Shabaab fighters exploded in the isolated hamlet of Illimey. The explosion injured a further two civilians, including an 18-month-old girl.[76]

This report shows that the US military can kill an eighteen-month-old girl in Somalia without any accountability and due process for the families. There has been very little outcry in US news media about these atrocities; in response, Somali activists have been at the forefront of exposing the murders of Somali civilians as a global component of the Black Lives Matter movement. Ifrah Hassan, a Somali college student, states that "the US media never talks about Somalis killed in US drone strikes; it has been young Somalis using social media that expose these atrocities."[77] Like Ifrah, a new generation of young Somalis is critiquing US empire from within. Therefore, the Somali diaspora has emerged as a vocal and visible critic of US imperialism. Yet this is the same diaspora that was made possible by US imperialism.

A February 2015 report published by the Anti-Defamation League lays bare the discursive work that the specter of Al-Shabaab does for the state. The report confidently states that "Americans began traveling to Somalia to join Al Shabab in 2007, around the time the group stepped up its insurgency against Somalia's transitional government and its Ethiopian supporters, who have since withdrawn. At least 50 US citizens and permanent residents are believed to have joined or attempted to join or aid the group since that time."[78] Al-Shabaab functions as a key character in an American drama that locates Muslims as disposable regardless of their affiliation with Al-Shabaab or their age, as was the case with the Somali child murdered by US drones. The state therefore links the foreign Al-Shabaab operating "over there" with the domestic Somalis being recruited by Al-Shabaab "over here." The state racializes Somalis as threats to both the domestic and global social order. Counterterrorism programs emerged as a response to this racialization of Muslims as terrorists. The development of counterterrorism programs within US police forces bespeaks the increasing intimacy between the military and the police; the SDPD's utilization of counterterrorism in particular underscores the translocal circuits of US imperial violence.[79] Abucar Guled, a young Somali refugee living in San Diego, explains, "As a young Somali person, I feel like people like me are under constant assault by the police, FBI, and US military because of the War on Terror and because of anti-Black racism. The US government targets Somalis in Somalia and Somalis in the diaspora too. Yet in school they tell me that America is the land of the free—I just don't buy it."[80]

As Abucar makes clear, the representation of the United States as beacon of freedom for refugees fleeing violence obscures the US militarism that produced and continues to haunt these refugee communities. The United States continues to represent itself as the yardstick against which the rest of the world is measured. US exceptionalism functions to legitimate US imperialism by disguising its nefarious activities under the guise of progress. In 1998, former president Bill Clinton claimed that "America is and will remain a target of terrorists precisely because we are leaders; because we act to advance peace, democracy, and basic human values; because we're the most open society on Earth; and because, as we have shown yet again, we take an uncompromising stand against *terrorism*."[81] Clinton utilized the language of colorblind racism by deploying race-neutral language to signal racial difference. The term "terrorist" in this speech functions as a code for Muslims. Islamophobia promotes the idea that Muslims cannot be saved through economic development or the civilizing mission of US intervention. This rhetoric encompasses America's reaction to Muslim refugees, who are viewed as incapable of assimilating American values. The most dramatic manifestation of this philosophy is Trump's ban on Muslim refugees, which resulted in a significant reduction in the number of refugees admitted into the United States. According to the US Department of State Bureau of Population, Refugees, and Migration, Muslim refugee admissions to the United States were cut by 91 percent between the years 2016 and 2018.[82]

Conclusion

In this chapter, I have critiqued the ways in which the state utilizes anti-Black racism and Islamophobia to justify military and police violence against Somalis. Centering the discussion on the Somali refugee community allows us to see that the historical and ongoing surveillance of Black communities in the United States is the condition of possibility for the surveillance of Muslims in the post-9/11 world.

I also emphasized the strategies Somalis employ to navigate and survive this surveillance. Juxtaposing a discursive reading of state documents and ethnographic counternarratives can reveal the complex interplay between power and resistance. The convergence of identities—Black/Muslim/refugee—is significant as a point of analysis because it reveals the multifaced ways in which structural racism and imperialism function in our present moment.

The Somali refugee community in San Diego numbers around thirty thousand; the country of Somalia, on the other hand, has a population of eighteen million.[83] Why have such a small country and refugee community attracted so much unwanted state surveillance and violent action? I argue that Somali refugees have become central figures in national security narratives because the state violence Somalis experience represents the convergence of anti-Black racism, Islamophobia, and nativism. The War on Drugs, as a mobilization of state resources from the 1970s to our present moment, would not have gained as much traction without the central role of anti-Black racism and the myth of the Black criminal as a governing ideology. The discourse of Islamophobia governs the War on Terror and the US military's excursions into Muslim-majority nations. Somali stories of resistance illuminate the ways in which domestic police brutality and US military violence abroad converge to produce an increasingly authoritarian state.

Conclusion

Somali Refugee Youths and Black Freedom, Summer 2020

In the summer of 2020, the Somali refugee community in the United States was once again confronted with the spectacle of police violence. The police murder of George Floyd that took place in Minneapolis galvanized the Somali community.[1] Amina Nur, a Somali activist in the BLM movement in Minneapolis, declared, "In Minneapolis, Somalis are fed up with the police, we deserve to live, and we deserve to thrive."[2] The Somali refugee community in Minneapolis emerged as the political epicenter of Somali activism in America. This is because Minneapolis has the largest Somali refugee population in the United States.[3] Months after the police murder of George Floyd, a young Somali man by the name of Dolal Idd was shot and killed by the police in December 2020.[4] Yet the lack of media attention to Dolal's murder highlights Somali refugees' relative invisibility around narratives of police violence against Black people. His murder also represents Somalis disproportionate encounters with the carceral state in the United States, a country to which Somalis fled to escape state violence. Somali refugees are arrested, racially profiled, and incarcerated at significantly higher rates relative to their population.[5] The intensity with which the carceral state has targeted Somalis was equally matched by the fervor of Somali activism and resistance in the summer of 2020. As a young Somali activist in San Diego named Yasmin exclaimed, "We refuse to be passive in the face of violence against our community. If all Black lives matter, then Black, immigrant lives need to matter too."[6]

Yasmin locates the Somali refugee struggle within the centuries-long Black freedom struggle in America, as theorized by Robin Kelley, who urges us to "take a long, hard look at our own surreality as well as surrealist thought and practice in order to build new movements, new possibilities, new conceptions of liberation."[7] As Yasmin elucidated, Somali refugees add new possibilities to the Black freedom struggle by insisting that immigrant rights are also fundamental concerns for the Black freedom struggle. Moreover, the BLM movement is inherently global because Black people are disproportionately killed by the US state apparatuses of violence not only in America but throughout the world.[8] As numerous Somali activists have pointed out, Black people are also killed by the US military in Somalia and held in detention centers by ICE, or Immigration and Customs Enforcement. Aisha, a Somali refugee activist in San Diego, highlighted this when she said that "US militarism is a Black problem, immigrant detention is a Black problem, and Somalis are at the forefront of exposing the connection between these issues in America."[9]

The framing of immigrant detention as a solely Latinx issue has been contested by Somali activists like Aisha, who have pointed to the high deportation and detention rates experienced by Black immigrants in the United States. According to Reema Ghabra, an immigration lawyer and fellow in the Black Immigrant and Refugee Equity (BIRE) project, "Black immigrants in [ICE] detention were more likely to have lengthier detentions and were six times more likely to be sent to solitary confinement."[10] Somali activists have also emphasized that police violence against Black people is not only a domestic issue but a form of state violence that affects Black people throughout the global diaspora. Therefore, resistance to anti-Blackness also needs to articulate a global agenda that is attentive to the ways anti-Black racism manifests internationally, as well as locally. Rinaldo Walcott describes this global anti-Blackness as a logic "that produce Black beings as nonhuman. The work is to make that claim foundational for Black diaspora studies/thought because it is, in fact, the various ways in which deployments of Western conceptions of the human function that continue to be the basis from which diasporic sensibilities, consciousness, and a potential politics might arise."[11] This vision to challenge global anti-Blackness was articulated by a group of Somali high school students in San Diego who took leadership positions in the BLM movement. In the summer of 2020, I cofounded a critical Somali studies collective with professors Jesse Mills and Udbi Ali that brought together a group of Somali activists and intellectuals from the San Diego Somali community. We envisioned convening this collective because we believed that Somali refugee youths were going through a political awakening in the midst of the BLM movement of 2020. During one of our Zoom sessions with a group of Somali high-school students and activists, I marveled at the energy with which these young refugees challenged global white supremacy. They were challenging the racism in their classrooms, the whiteness of the curriculum, and the over-policing of their neighborhoods.

These students were advocating for police abolition and envisioning a radically different society than the one they inherited. Meeting these young activists, and being part of the BLM movement myself, gave life to the themes I addressed in this book. I wrote this book to interrogate Somali refugees' experiences with and resistance to state violence. I looked at the impact of policing in the lives of Somali refugees, from the Dadaab refugee camp in Kenya to City Heights, San Diego. Therefore, this book adds to the growing scholarship on policing and anti-Blackness by providing a global and comparative analysis of Black people's lived experiences with police violence.

Somali refugees utilize their intimate experiences with state violence to reveal the interconnected relationship between police violence domestically and US military violence abroad. There is a disconnect between scholars who study US militarism[12] and those who study the carceral state,[13] and my book bridges this gap by showing that the emergence of militarized policing is a function of US imperialism. I do so by centering the experiences and embodied knowledge of Somali refugees who have traversed the circuits of US empire, from Somalia to Kenya to San Diego.

Somali refugees' lived experiences are an embodied knowledge that illuminates the links between police violence against Black people in the United States and US military violence against Black people abroad. The testimony of Fahima Hassan, a young Somali activist in San Diego, powerfully embodies this connection: "My brother was assaulted by the police in San Diego and my uncle killed by US drone strikes in Somalia."[14] Fahima's story shows the growing threat US militarism poses to Black life globally. The US military is expanding its presence on the African continent, with twenty-nine US military bases in Africa as of 2020.[15] Therefore it becomes increasingly important for the BLM movement to take an international approach to state violence against Black people. Ahmed Ali, a Somali refugee activist based in Los Angeles, pushes this point: "As a BLM organizer I try to articulate to my fellow organizers that we need to look at violence against Black people as a global issue."[16] The devaluation of Black life is not an issue limited to the United States; it also impacts the Black diaspora writ large. As Mariame Makabe and Andrea Ritchie argue, "Given the role of the US military as global police, defund demands are deeply connected to global struggles against settler colonialism, militarism, and imperialism, and for migrant justice."[17] Somali activists provide an important lens through which to view Black resistance to state violence, as they mobilize a translocal politics that reveals how state violence at the local level is informed by state violence internationally.

The partnership between the US military and the San Diego Police Department best highlights this phenomenon. The SDPD utilizes intelligence gathered by the US military during their operations in Somalia.[18] Armed with this intel, the SDPD counterterrorism task force has claimed that Al-Shabaab, a terrorist organization located in Somalia, is recruiting Somali youths in San Diego. Therefore, the racialization of Somalis as terrorist threats links Somalis in Somalia to Somalis in San Diego as two populations that need to be surveilled and at times eliminated by the state. The emergence of counterterrorism programs in police departments throughout the country signals the carceral state's increasingly militarized and global approach.

Moreover, it also shows that racial discourses such as Islamophobia travel along the same circuits as US imperialism, from San Diego to Somalia and back. I showed this trend in chapter 2, where I analyzed the ways in which police in Kenya use Islamophobia to rationalize a security state apparatus that targets Somalis for racial profiling and state surveillance. Islamophobia is the guiding structure for surveilling Somalis both in Kenya and the United States. The Kenyan police and the SDPD both cite the threat of terrorism as justification for surveilling the Somali refugee community in their respective countries.

The emergence of counterterrorism programs within police forces has accelerated the militarization of police departments because police forces are provided military equipment to combat the threat of domestic terrorism. According to Stuart Schrader, "These institutions represented three unpopular positions: a turn toward counterinsurgency, a shift away from prioritizing the military to wage counterinsurgency, and the centralization of oversight of counterinsurgency into one council. They transformed counterinsurgency into policing."[19] Schrader underscores the historical precedent for the global reach of US police by examining the career of the "father of US foreign police assistance," Kansas City police officer Byron Engel, observing, "Engle's cop cohort figured their project of police reform as a global one."[20] The War on Drugs also represented a moment in which police took a global approach to combatting drug traffickers. My contribution to this conversation is to link the War on Drugs with the War on Terror by highlighting the racial discourses of anti-Blackness and Islamophobia that are deployed to legitimize state violence and the militarization of the police.

The enduring legacies of the War on Drugs and War on Terror highlight the dual transformation of the military and police. The police have increasingly taken a more global approach with the emergence of counterterrorism. In 2015, Minnesota Police Chief John Harrington traveled to Somalia to teach Somali police forces how to fight terrorism.[21] This police chief's visit signals US police forces' recent global orientation as a result of the War on Terror, revealing how Somali refugees and the nation of Somalia have increasingly become targets in this war.

The US military has also focused inward, with an emphasis on domestic issues, by providing military equipment to police forces.[22] By juxtaposing Somali refugees' lived experience with a discourse analysis of police and military documents, I have shown that racial narratives of criminality and terrorism are central to the expansion of both US militarism and the carceral state. The Somali refugee community has been deemed a threat both in Kenya and the United States due to the discourse of terrorism that marks Somali refugees as dangerous.[23] For the Somali refugee community, Islamophobia cannot be analytically separated from anti-Black racism. As Somali refugees, we cannot compartmentalize our identities but must navigate a world that deems Black life and Muslim life as disposable.

The Somali refugee experience in Kenya mirrors the Somali refugee experience in the United States in many ways, but it differs in profound ways as well. One key difference is that in America there is a clear path to citizenship for Somali refugees, whereas in Kenya Somali refugees are often barred from citizenship. Omar, a Somali refugee living in Kenya, was told "he did not qualify for citizenship because his fingerprints were in the refugee database."[24] A similarity the United States and Kenya share is the practice of detaining refugee children. Somali refugees in Dadaab are held in refugee camps, where barbed wire separates Somali refugees from the rest of Kenyan society, a practice that preceded Donald Trump's policy of caging immigrant children in detention centers around the United States.[25] Another feature that Kenya shares with the United States is hostility to Somali refugees. In Kenya the standard official narrative is that Somali refugees are a threat to Kenyan society and a drain on Kenya's resources. As former Kenyan president

Mwai Kibaki stated in 2012: "Kenya can no longer continue carrying the Somali burden." As a response to this Somali "burden" in 2019, the Kenyan government made plans to build a $35 million border wall between Kenya and Somalia, mirroring Trump's promise to build a wall between Mexico and the United States.[26]

The Somali refugee experience with state violence is instructive because it shows that Islamophobic, anti-immigrant, and anti-Black rhetoric work in tandem to buttress an increasingly carceral and militarized state. The Trump administration regularly mobilized hateful rhetoric around immigrants, Muslims, and Black people, all the while creating policies that disadvantaged these groups. Yet the issues affecting Muslims, immigrants, and Black people are often viewed as separate and distinct. Therefore, groups that advocate for these communities are at times siloed off. The Somali refugee experience reveals that anti-Black racism buttresses Islamophobia, and anti-immigrant rhetoric mirrors anti-Blackness. This was best encapsulated by Trump's characterization of Mexican immigrants in 2018 "as rapists and drug dealers."[27] This trope draws from the long legacy of criminalizing Black people as a means to maintain the borders of the Jim Crow South.[28] As Black Studies scholar Treva Lindsey elucidates, "Postslavery, it was Jim Crow laws, as well as the creative remixing of bondage practices and criminalizing and racist and sexist ideologies, that rendered Black people in the United States distinctly vulnerable to carceral technologies, systems, and institutions."[29] The racial policing of borders is utilized today to maintain the borders between Mexico and the United States, dictating who deserves to be in this country and who does not.

The Somali refugee experience shows that policing is not just an issue that impacts Black people. Moreover, the same police who murder Black people are working with a US military regime that murders Muslims. State violence is multifaced and transnational; as a result, resistance to state violence also needs to be multifaced and transnational. The protests that took place all over the world as a response to the police murder of George Floyd hint at the emergence of a Black transnational social movement for racial justice. In the words of Aisha, a young Somali refugee activist, "I believe in a future without state violence against Black people, and that future is Black, global, and immigrant centric."[30]

Notes

Introduction

1. *The Other Epidemic: Fatal Police Shootings in the Time of COVID-19* (ACLU research report, August 18, 2020), 4, https://www.aclu.org/report/other-epidemic-fatal-police-shootings-time-covid-19.

2. Elisabeth Gawthrop, "The Color of Coronavirus: Covid-19 Deaths Analyzed by Race and Ethnicity in the US," Color of Coronavirus Project: Key Findings, APM Research Lab, October 19, 2023, https://www.apmresearchlab.org/covid/deaths-by-race.

3. Tari Ajadi and Debra Thompson, "The Two Pandemics of Anti-Black Racism and COVID-19 Are Tied Together," *The Globe and Mail*, May 22, 2021, https://www.theglobeandmail.com/opinion/article-the-two-pandemics-of-anti-black-racism-and-covid-19-are-tied-together/.

4. Christina Sharpe, *In the Wake: On Blackness and Being* (Durham, NC: Duke University Press, 2016), 13.

5. Khalil Gibran Muhammad, *The Condemnation of Blackness: Race, Crime, and the Making of Modern Urban America* (Cambridge, MA: Harvard University Press, 2019).

6. Mari Payton, Dorian Hargrove, Tom Jones, and Jay Yoo, "La Mesa Police Release Timeline of May 30 Demonstration," NBC 7 San Diego, June 9, 2020, https://www.nbcsandiego.com/news/investigations/la-mesa-police-release-timeline-of-may-30-demonstration/2343500/.

7. Boutros Boutros-Ghali, introduction to *The United Nations and Somalia, 1992–1996* (New York: United Nations Department of Public Information, 1996), 45.

8. Abdi Mohamed Kusow, "The Genesis of the Somali Civil War: A New Perspective," *Northeast African Studies* 1, no. 1 (1994): 31–46.

9. Drew DeSilver, "How the US Compares with Other Countries Taking in Refugees," Pew Research Center, September 24, 2015, https://www.pewresearch.org/fact-tank/2015/09/24/how-the-u-s-compares-with-other-countries-taking-in-refugees/.

10. "UN-Run Camps for Somalia Refugees in Kenya Enter 20th Year of Existence," UN News, February 21, 2012, https://news.un.org/en/story/2012/02/404012.

11. "UN-Run Camps for Somalia Refugees in Kenya."

12. "Protracted Refugee Situations Explained," USA for UNHCR, January 28, 2020, https://www.unrefugees.org/news/protracted-refugee-situations-explained/.

13. "UN-Run Camps for Somalia Refugees."

14. "Dadaab Refugee Complex," UNHCR Kenya, https://www.unhcr.org/ke/dadaab-refugee-complex.

15. "Terrorism in Somalia: Al-Shabaab Continues Deadly Attacks," Vision of Humanity, https://www.visionofhumanity.org/country-close-up-terrorism-in-somalia/.

16. Long Bui, "The Refugee Repertoire: Performing and Staging the Postmemories of Violence," *MELUS* 41, no. 3 (2016): 112.

17. Somali Family Service of San Diego, Candid, GuideStar Profile, 2022, https://www.guidestar.org/profile/91-2065038.

18. I borrow the term *militarized refuge* from Yến Lê Espiritu, *Body Counts: The Vietnam War and Militarized Refuge(es)* (Oakland: University of California Press, 2014).

19. Mary Lang, "Somali Refugees Make Their Way in San Diego," *San Diego Reader*, February 18, 1993, https://www.sandiegoreader.com/news/1993/feb/18/home-dark/.

20. Elizabeth Aguilera, "San Diego Welcomes More Refugees than Any Other California County," CalMatters, July 20, 2017, https://calmatters.org/justice/2017/07/san-diego-welcomes-refugees-california-county/.

21. Linda Borgen and Rubén Rumbaut, "Coming of Age in 'America's Finest City': Transitions to Adulthood among Children of Immigrants in San Diego," in *Coming of Age in America: The Transition to Adulthood in the Twenty-*

First Century, eds. Mary C. Waters, Patrick J. Carr, Maria J. Kefalas, and Jennifer Holdaway (Berkeley: University of California Press, 2011), 138.

22. "About Refugee Admissions," United States Department of State, https://www.state.gov/refugee-admissions/about/.

23. Jesse Mills, "Racing to Refuge: Ethnicity, Gendered Violence, and Somali Youth in San Diego" (PhD diss., University of California, San Diego, 2008), 14.

24. Office of Refugee Resettlement, "Who We Serve—Refugees," Administration for Children and Families, US Department of Health and Human Services, March 16, 2022, https://www.acf.hhs.gov/orr/policy-guidance/who-we-serve-refugees.

25. San Diego Tourism Authority, "Military Information: From Bases to the USO to Public Affairs Offices," San Diego.org, 2023, https://www.sandiego.org/articles/military/military-information.aspx.

26. Abraham J. Shragge, "'I Like the Cut of Your Jib': Cultures of Accommodation between the US Navy and Citizens of San Diego, California, 1900–1951," *Journal of San Diego History* 48, no. 3 (Summer 2002), https://sandiegohistory.org/journal/2002/july/navy-2/.

27. Robert Dietrich and Wayne Carlson, "Pendleton—New Horizon for Refugees," in "From the Archive: April 30, 1975: Refugees Arrive at Camp Pendleton," *San Diego Union-Tribune*, April 30, 2018, https://www.sandiegouniontribune.com/news/150-years/sd-me-150-years-april-30-htmlstory.html.

28. Interview with Sumeya Farah, San Diego, California, November 2019.

29. Andrew G. Mills and Joseph R. Clark, "Running a Three-Legged Race: The San Diego Police Department, the Intelligence Community, and Counterterrorism," Homeland Security Policy Institute, George Washington University, brief 12, August 1, 2011, https://www.jstor.org/stable/resrep20744.

30. "Three Somali Immigrants Sentenced for Providing Support to Foreign Terrorists," press release, FBI, San Diego Division, November 18, 2013, https://archives.fbi.gov/archives/sandiego/press-releases/2013/three-somali-immigrants-sentenced-for-providing-support-to-foreign-terrorists.

31. "Joint Terrorism Task Forces," FBI, June 13, 2016. https://www.fbi.gov/investigate/terrorism/joint-terrorism-task-forces.

32. Lyndsay Winkley and Teri Figueroa, "San Diego Has More than 3,000 Cameras on Streetlights. Are All Neighborhoods Treated Equally?" *San Diego*

Union-Tribune, March 1, 2020, https://www.sandiegouniontribune.com/news/public-safety/story/2020-03-01/san-diego-has-3-000-cameras-on-street-lights-do-they-target-any.

33. Interview with Hodan Yusuf, San Diego, California, February 2018.

34. Interview with Aisha Abdullahi, San Diego, California, October 2020.

35. Monica Anderson, "African Immigrant Population in US Steadily Climbs," Pew Research Center, February 14, 2017, https://www.pewresearch.org/fact-tank/2017/02/14/african-immigrant-population-in-u-s-steadily-climbs/.

36. Tod G. Hamilton, *Immigration and the Remaking of Black America* (New York: Russell Sage Foundation, 2019).

37. Aaron Terrazas, "African Immigrants in the United States in 2007," Migration Policy Institute, July 16, 2020, https://www.migrationpolicy.org/article/african-immigrants-united-states-2007#6.

38. Frank Wilderson III, "Gramsci's Black Marx: Whither the Slave in Civil Society?" *Social Identities* 9, no. 2 (2003): 225–40; Jared Sexton, "People-of-Color-Blindness: Notes on the Afterlife of Slavery," *Social Text* 28, no. 2 (2010): 31–56; Saidiya V. Hartman, *Scenes of Subjection Terror, Slavery, and Self-Making in Nineteenth-Century America* (New York: Norton, 2022); Hortense J. Spillers, *Black, White, and in Color: Essays on American Literature and Culture* (Chicago: University of Chicago Press, 2003); Sharpe, *In the Wake*.

39. Michelle M. Wright, *Physics of Blackness: Beyond the Middle Passage Epistemology* (Minneapolis: University of Minnesota Press, 2015), 8.

40. Roderick A. Ferguson, "The Lateral Moves of African American Studies in a Period of Migration," in *Strange Affinities: The Gender and Sexual Politics of Comparative Racialization*, eds. Grace Kyungwon Hong and Roderick A. Ferguson (Durham, NC: Duke University Press, 2011), 117.

41. Edward E. Curtis, "African-American Islamization Reconsidered: Black History Narratives and Muslim Identity," *Journal of the American Academy of Religion* 73, no. 3 (2005): 659–84.

42. Su'ad Abdul Khabeer, *Muslim Cool: Race, Religion, and Hip Hop in the United States* (New York: NYU Press, 2016), 69.

43. *Muslim Americans: No Signs of Growth in Alienation or Support for Extremism* (Pew Research Center report, August 30, 2011), https://www.pewresearch.org/politics/2011/08/30/muslim-americans-no-signs-of-growth-in-alienation-or-support-for-extremism/.

44. Muriam Haleh Davis, "'Incommensurate Ontologies'? Anti-Black Racism and the Question of Islam in French Algeria," *Lateral* 10, no. 1 (2021).
45. Wilderson, "Gramsci's Black Marx," 237–38.
46. Interview with Suada Nur, San Diego, California, September 2020.
47. Donna Auston, "Prayer, Protest, and Police Brutality: Black Muslim Spiritual Resistance in the Ferguson Era," *Transforming Anthropology* 25, no. 1 (2017): 14.
48. Dylan Rodriguez, *Forced Passages: Imprisoned Radical Intellectuals and the US Prison Regime* (Minneapolis: University of Minnesota Press, 2006); Muhammad, *The Condemnation of Blackness*; Michelle Alexander, *The New Jim Crow: Mass Incarceration in the Age of Colorblindness* (New York: The New Press, 2020); Ruth Wilson Gilmore, *Golden Gulag: Prisons, Surplus, Crisis, and Opposition in Globalizing California* (Berkeley: University of California Press, 2007); Mimi Thi Nguyen, *The Gift of Freedom: War, Debt, and Other Refugee Passages* (Durham, NC: Duke University Press, 2012).
49. Espiritu, *Body Counts*; Simeon Man, *Soldiering through Empire: Race and the Making of the Decolonizing Pacific* (Oakland: University of California Press, 2018).
50. Sanya Mansoor, "'At the Intersection of Two Criminalized Identities': Black and Non-Black Muslims Confront a Complicated Relationship with Policing and Anti-Blackness," *Time*, September 15, 2020, https://time.com/5884176/islam-black-lives-matter-policing-muslims/.
51. Espiritu, *Body Counts*, 2.

Chapter 1. US Imperialism and Somali Refugees

1. "The Somalia Mission; Clinton's Words on Somalia: 'The Responsibilities of American Leadership,'" Reuters via *New York Times*, October 8, 1993, https://www.nytimes.com/1993/10/08/world/somalia-mission-clinton-s-words-somalia-responsibilities-american-leadership.html.
2. Pew Research Center estimates the total number of Somali refugees living in a "temporary refugee situation" from 1990 to 2014 increased from 450,000 to 1.1 million. See Phillip Connor and Jens Krogstad, "5 Facts about the Global Somali Diaspora," Pew Research Center, June 1, 2016, https://www.pewresearch.org/short-reads/2016/06/01/5-facts-about-the-global-somali-diaspora/.

3. Interview with Aisha Ahmed, San Diego, California, October 2016.

4. Wang Shih-tsung, "The Conference of Berlin and British 'New' Imperialism, 1884–85," manuscript, National Taiwan University, 1998, https://scholars.lib.ntu.edu.tw/handle/123456789/4678.

5. "General Act of the Berlin Conference on West Africa," February 26, 1885, https://loveman.sdsu.edu/docs/1885GeneralActBerlinConference.pdf.

6. Walter Rodney, *How Europe Underdeveloped Africa* (Washington, DC: Howard University Press, 1982), 160.

7. Interview with Sumeya Hassan, San Diego, California, May 12, 2018.

8. Interview with Ahmed Ali, San Diego, California, December 20, 2019.

9. Donna R. Jackson, *US Foreign Policy in the Horn of Africa: From Colonialism to Terrorism* (London: Routledge, 2017), 135–52.

10. "Disposal of the Italian Colonies," memorandum by the secretary of state for foreign affairs, April 18, 1946, National Archives, Kew, UK, http://filestore.nationalarchives.gov.uk/pdfs/large/cab-129-10.pdf.

11. See "Issa Somali [1914]," in the web archive titled, "Let Me Get There: Visualizing Immigrants, Transnational Migrants & US Citizens Abroad, 1904–1925," compiled by Louis Takács, https://scalar.usc.edu/works/let-me-get-there/issa-somali-1914.

12. Interview with Nasra Hussein, San Diego, California, March 2018.

13. W. B., "What Is Happening to Africa's Pirates?" *The Economist*, January 16, 2018, https://www.economist.com/the-economist-explains/2018/01/16/what-is-happening-to-africas-pirates.

14. Ghazi Abuhakema and Tim Carmichael, "The Somali Youth League Constitution: A Handwritten Arabic Copy (c. 1947?) from the Ethiopian Security Forces Archives in Harär," *Journal of Eastern African Studies* 4, no. 3 (2010): 450–66.

15. "Trusteeship Agreement for the Territory of Somaliland under Italian Administration, Adopted by the Trusteeship Council, January 27, 1950," *International Organization* 4, no. 2 (1950): 347–56.

16. Safia Aidid, "*Haweenku Wa Garab* (Women Are a Force): Women and the Somali Nationalist Movement, 1943–1960," *Bildhaan: An International Journal of Somali Studies* 10 (2010): 105.

17. Gilbert Ware, "Somalia: From Trust Territory to Nation, 1950–1960," *Phylon* 26, no. 2 (1965): 173.

18. Abdi Ismail Samatar, *Africa's First Democrats: Somalia's Aden A. Osman and Abdirazak H. Hussen* (Bloomington: Indiana University Press, 2016), 18.

19. Achille Mbembe, *On the Postcolony* (Berkeley: University of California Press, 2001), 31.

20. "Trusteeship Agreement," 348.

21. Interview with Ali Abucar, San Diego, California, April 2019.

22. E. R. Turton, "Somali Resistance to Colonial Rule and the Development of Somali Political Activity in Kenya 1893-1960," *Journal of African History* 13, no. 1 (1972): 121.

23. Abdi Ismail Samatar and Ahmed I. Samatar, "Somalis as Africa's First Democrats: Premier Abdirazak H. Hussein and President Aden A. Osman," *Bildhaan: An International Journal of Somali Studies* 2 (2002): 23.

24. Interview with Abdinasir Nur, San Diego, California, June 2016.

25. Interview with Ahmed Kusow, San Diego, California, February 2016.

26. Cawo M. Abdi, *Elusive Jannah: The Somali Diaspora and a Borderless Muslim Identity* (Minneapolis: University of Minnesota Press, 2015), 34.

27. "British Somalis, the Ogaden," Official Reports of Debates in UK Parliament, November 1955, https://api.parliament.uk/historic-hansard/commons/1955/nov/17/british-somalis-the-ogaden.

28. Interview with Aisha Osman, San Diego, California, January 2017.

29. Quoted in Odd Arne Westad, *The Global Cold War* (Cambridge: Cambridge University Press, 2006), 283.

30. Quoted in Westad, *The Global Cold War*, 284.

31. "President Ronald Reagan's Meeting with President Mohammed Siad Barre of Somalia. Oval Office," video recording, March 11, 1982, National Archives: Records of the White House Television Office, https://catalog.archives.gov/id/66383776.

32. Mohamed Haji Ingiriis, *The Suicidal State in Somalia: The Rise and Fall of the Siad Barre Regime, 1969-1991* (Lanham, MD: University Press of America, 2016), 34.

33. Abdi Sheik-Abdi, "Ideology and Leadership in Somalia," *Journal of Modern African Studies* 19, no. 1 (1981): 163-72.

34. Interview with Aisha Hussein, San Diego, California, May 2018.

35. Mohamed Haji Ingiriis, "How Somalia Works: Mimicry and the Making of Mohamed Siad Barre's Regime in Mogadishu," *Africa Today* 63, no. 1 (2016): 57-73.

36. Mehari Taddele Maru, "The Future of Somalia's Legal System and Its Contribution to Peace and Development," *Journal of Peacebuilding & Development* 4, no. 1 (2008): 1–15.

37. Ingiriis, "How Somalia Works," 62. And see Alice Bettis Hashim, *The Fallen State: Dissonance, Dictatorship, and Death in Somalia* (Lanham, MD: University Press of America, 1997), 5.

38. Patrick Gilkes, "Somalia: Conflicts within and against the Military Regime," *Review of African Political Economy* 16, no. 44 (1989): 53–58.

39. Interview with Omar Hussein, San Diego, California, August 2019.

40. James Scott, in the text of *Domination and the Arts of Resistance: Hidden Transcripts* (New Haven, CT: Yale University Press, 2009), defines infrapolitics as the everyday modes of resistance deployed by the most vulnerable in society.

41. Amnesty International, *Annual Report 1989* (London: Amnesty International Publications, 1989), https://www.amnesty.org/en/documents/pol10/0002/1989/en/.

42. Ken Menkhaus, "US Foreign Assistance to Somalia: Phoenix from the Ashes?" *Middle East Policy* 5, no. 1 (1997): 124–49.

43. Peter J. Schraeder, "The Horn of Africa: US Foreign Policy in an Altered Cold War Environment," *Middle East Journal* 46, no. 4 (1992): 571.

44. Catherine Lowe Besteman, *Making Refuge: Somali Bantu Refugees and Lewiston, Maine* (Durham, NC: Duke University Press, 2016), 45.

45. Besteman, *Making Refuge*, 45.

46. "Horn of Africa," document dated September 18, 1980, in Subcommittee on Human Resources, *Unauthorized Transfers of Nonpublic Information During the 1980 Presidential Election*, House of Representatives (Washington, DC: Government Printing Office, 1984), 727.

47. Donna R. Jackson, "The Carter Administration and Somalia," *Diplomatic History* 31, no. 4 (2007): 29.

48. Jeffrey Alan Lefebvre, *Arms for the Horn: US Security Policy in Ethiopia and Somalia, 1953–1991* (Pittsburgh, PA: University of Pittsburgh Press, 1992).

49. For more on the motivations for Barre's war with Ethiopia in 1977, see Harry Odada, "Somalia's Domestic Politics and Foreign Relations since the Ogaden War of 1977–78," *Middle Eastern Studies* 21, no. 3 (1985): 285–97.

50. Tibebe Eshete, "Towards a History of the Incorporation of the Ogaden: 1887–1935," *Journal of Ethiopian Studies* 27, no. 2 (1994): 69–87.

51. Kenneth G. Weiss, "The Soviet Involvement in the Ogaden War," Center for Naval Analyses, professional paper 269, February 1, 1980, Defense Technical Information Center, https://apps.dtic.mil/sti/citations/ADA082219.

52. Interview with Ali Hussein, San Diego, California, March 2019.

53. Terry Atlas, "Cold War Rivals Sowed Seeds of Somalia Tragedy," *Chicago Tribune*, December 13, 1992, https://www.chicagotribune.com/news/ct-xpm-1992-12-13-9204230505-story.html.

54. Besteman, *Making Refuge*, 44.

55. Interview with Amina Hassan, San Diego, California, February 2016.

56. Amnesty International, *Annual Report 1989*, 84.

57. Interview with Abdi Hassan, San Diego, California, November 2018.

58. Mary L. Dudziak, *Cold War Civil Rights: Race and the Image of American Democracy* (Princeton, NJ: Princeton University Press, 2011).

59. Lefebvre, *Arms for the Horn*, 202.

60. Lidwien Kapteijns, *Clan Cleansing in Somalia: The Ruinous Legacy of 1991* (Philadelphia: University of Pennsylvania Press, 2013), 94.

61. Lefebvre, *Arms for the Horn*, 201.

62. See Mohammed Ibrahim Shire, *Somali President, Mohammed Siad Barre: His Life and Legacy* (Leicester, UK: Cirfe Publications, 2011).

63. Interview with Asha Ahmed, San Diego, California, March 2017.

64. In *Clan Cleansing in Somalia*, Lidwien Kapteijns reduces the Somali civil war to clan conflict and ignores the role of US militarism and British colonialism in creating and exacerbating the conflict in Somalia.

65. Nikki Tundel, "Somali-Americans Who Fled Civil War Confront Tribalism in New Home," MPR News, Minneapolis, June 5, 2014, https://www.mprnews.org/story/2014/06/05/somali-anti-tribalism.

66. See Abdi, *Elusive Jannah*.

67. Interview with Faysal Ahmed, San Diego, California, March 2018.

68. David Vine, *The United States of War: A Global History of America's Endless Conflicts, from Columbus to the Islamic State* (Oakland: University of California Press, 2020).

69. Interview with Ahmed Ali, San Diego, California, August 2019.

70. Boutros Boutros-Ghali, "Report of the Secretary-General on the Situation in Somalia, Proposing the Expansion of UNOSOM and the Creation of Four Operational Zones," July 22, 1992, in *The United Nations and Somalia, 1992–1996* (New York: United Nations Department of Public Information, 1996), 178.

71. Interview with Ali Hussein, San Diego, California, May 2018.

72. The World Bank, *Conflict in Somalia: Drivers and Dynamics* (The World Bank, 2005), 11, http://www.jstor.org/stable/resrep02475.

73. Boutros-Ghali, introduction to *The United Nations and Somalia 1992–1996*, 17.

74. Neda Atanasoski, *Humanitarian Violence: The US Deployment of Diversity* (Minneapolis: University of Minnesota Press, 2013).

75. Dennis P. Mroczkowski, *Restoring Hope: In Somalia with the Unified Task Force, 1992–1993* (Washington, DC: History Division, United States Marine Corps, 2005), 11.

76. Bernard C. Cohen, "A View from the Academy," in *Taken by Storm: The Media, Public Opinion, and US Foreign Policy in the Gulf War*, eds. W. Lance Bennett and David L. Paletz (Chicago: University of Chicago Press, 1994), 9–10.

77. Austine E. Iyare, "Suffering and the Encounter of the Other in African Spaces," in *Handbook of African Philosophy of Difference*, ed. Elvis Imafidon (Cham: Springer, 2020), 289–99.

78. "1992: American Marines Land in Somalia," *On this Day*, BBC News, December 9, 1992, http://news.bbc.co.uk/onthisday/hi/dates/stories/december/9/newsid_4013000/4013143.stm.

79. Mroczkowski, *Restoring Hope*, 12.

80. Boutros-Ghali, "Further Report of the Secretary-General . . . ,"August 17, 1993, in *The United Nations and Somalia 1992–1996*, 279–80.

81. Interview with Amina Sheik, San Diego, California, May 2018.

82. Boutros-Ghali, "Report of the Secretary-General," July 22, 1992, in *The United Nations and Somalia 1992–1996*, 173.

83. Boutros-Ghali, "Report of the Secretary-General," 173.

84. Boutros-Ghali, "Report of the Secretary-General," 173.

85. Terry Atlas, "Cold War Rivals Sowed Seeds of Somalia Tragedy," *Chicago Tribune*, December 13, 1992, https://www.chicagotribune.com/news/ct-xpm-1992-12-13-9204230505-story.html.

86. Interview with Hamdi Nur, San Diego, California, June 2019.

87. Boutros-Ghali, "Letter Dated 24 November 1992 . . . ," November 27, 1992, in *The United Nations and Somalia 1992–1996*, 207.

88. Interview with Asho Noor, San Diego, California, April 2019.

89. Boutros-Ghali, introduction to *The United Nations and Somalia 1992–1996*, 33.

90. Interview with Faysal Ahmed, San Diego, California, March 2018.

91. Kapteijns, *Clan Cleansing*, 167.

92. *Black Hawk Down*, directed by Ridley Scott, Columbia Pictures, January 18, 2002, https://www.imdb.com/title/tt0265086/.

93. Stephen A. Klien, "Public Character and the Simulacrum: The Construction of the Soldier Patriot and Citizen Agency in *Black Hawk Down*," *Critical Studies in Media Communication* 22, no. 5 (2005): 427–49.

94. Interview with Ayaab Jamac, San Diego, California, March 2018.

95. The United Nations High Commissioner for Refugees lists the total refugee population at 79.5 million as of June 2020.

96. Abdi, *Elusive Jannah*.

97. John Wilkens, "New Group of Refugees Finds Safe Haven Here," *San Diego Union-Tribune*, October 4, 1994.

98. Interview with Faduma Gure, San Diego, California, September 2017.

99. Allison Fedirka, "Why the US Cares about Somalia," Geopolitical Futures, May 10, 2017, https://geopoliticalfutures.com/us-cares-somalia/.

100. The PBS documentary *Somalia: A Nation of Poets* (aired August 11, 2017) highlights the significance of poetry to the Somali community both contemporarily and historically.

101. Aidid, "*Haweenku Wa Garab*," 109–10.

102. "Figures at a Glance," UNHCR Kenya, https://www.unhcr.org/ke/figures-at-a-glance.

Chapter 2. The Carceral Refugee Camp

1. Interview with Abdi Hamza, San Diego, California April 2017.

2. According to the United Nations High Commissioner for Refugees in Kenya, the Dadaab refugee camp has 218,873 refugees as of July 2020. See "Dadaab Refugee Complex," UNHCR Kenya, https://www.unhcr.org/ke/dadaab-refugee-complex.

3. Assadullah Nasrullah, "UN Refugee Chief in Dadaab Camps, Reassures Refugees, Returnees and Host Community of UNHCR's Support," UNHCR Kenya, December 21, 2017, https://www.unhcr.org/ke/12985-un-refugee-chief-dadaab-camps-reassures-refugees-returnees-host-community-unhcrs-support.html.

4. Interview with Hussein Ali, San Diego, California May 2018.

5. Gerry Simpson, "Somali Refugees in Kenya Forgotten and Abused," *The Standard*, republished by Human Rights Watch, March 31, 2009, https://www.hrw.org/news/2009/03/31/somali-refugees-kenya-forgotten-and-abused.

6. UNHCR, "Global Trends: Forced Displacement in 2015," UNHCR, 2015, https://www.unhcr.org/us/media/unhcr-global-trends-2015.

7. Marc-Antoine Perouse de Montclos and Peter Mwangi Kagwanja, "Refugee Camps or Cities? The Socio-Economic Dynamics of the Dadaab and Kakuma Camps in Northern Kenya," *Journal of Refugee Studies* 13, no. 2 (2000): 205.

8. Abel Bennett Holla, "Fractured Ties: Power Competition and Politics Influencing Security Strategies of Kenya and Somalia in the Horn of Africa Region," *Path of Science* 7, no. 6 (2021): 1010–15.

9. I. M. Lewis, "The Problem of the Northern Frontier District of Kenya," *Race* 5, no. 1 (1963): 48–60.

10. Interview with Abdi Nur, San Diego, California, November 2019.

11. Gerry Simpson, "'You Are All Terrorists': Kenyan Police Abuse of Refugees in Nairobi," Human Rights Watch, March 29, 2013, https://www.hrw.org/report/2013/05/29/you-are-all-terrorists/Kenyan-police-abuse-refugees-nairobi.

12. Catherine Lowe Besteman, *Making Refuge: Somali Bantu Refugees and Lewiston, Maine* (Durham, NC: Duke University Press, 2016), 65.

13. "The Refugees Act of 2006," Kenya, Act no. 13, sec. 14, International Humanitarian Law Database, 2006, https://ihl-databases.icrc.org/en/national-practice/refugees-act-2006-1.

14. Interview of Maryam Hassan, Columbus, Ohio, November 2019.

15. "The Refugees Act of 2006," Kenya, Act no. 13, sec. 14.

16. "Universal Declaration of Human Rights at 70: 30 Articles on 30 Articles—Article 13," UN OHCHR, November 22, 2018, https://www.ohchr.org/en/press-releases/2018/11/universal-declaration-human-rights-70-30-articles-30-articles-article-13?LangID=E&NewsID=23916.

17. Interview with Ladan Diriye, San Diego, California, September 2018.

18. Montclos and Kagwanja, "Refugee Camps or Cities?" 211–12.

19. "Kenya's Refugee Act 2021: Opportunities for Refugee Livelihoods and Self-Reliance, Part 1," Hebrew Immigrant Aid Soscieety, https://hias.org/wp-content/uploads/kenyas_refugee_act_2021-_opportunities_for_refugee_livelihoods_and_self-reliance_-final_draft31.pdf.

20. Mohammed Yusuf, "Kenyan Police Dogged by Extortion Charges," Al Jazeera, August 7, 2014, https://www.aljazeera.com/news/2014/8/7/kenyan-police-dogged-by-extortion-charges.

21. Simpson, "'You Are All Terrorists.'"

22. Interview with Hamdi Ali, San Diego, California, April 2018.

23. "Refugee Act," no. 10 of 2021, sec. 41(1)b, Kenya Law database, December 3, 2021. http://kenyalaw.org:8181/exist/kenyalex/actview.xql?actid=No.+10+of+2021.

24. Interview with Hamdi Ali, San Diego, California, April 2018.

25. Gerry Simpson, "'Welcome to Kenya': Police Abuse of Somali Refugees," Human Rights Watch, June 17, 2010, https://www.hrw.org/report/2010/06/17/welcome-kenya/police-abuse-somali-refugees.

26. "Kenya: Involuntary Refugee Returns to Somalia," Human Rights Watch, September 14, 2016, https://www.hrw.org/news/2016/09/15/kenya-involuntary-refugee-returns-somalia.

27. Interview with Safia Musa, San Diego, California March 2019.

28. Neda Atanasoski, *Humanitarian Violence: The US Deployment of Diversity* (Minneapolis: University of Minnesota Press, 2013), 2.

29. "WFP/UNHCR Guidelines for Estimating: Food and Nutritional Needs in Emergencies," UNHCR, December 1997, paragraph 1, https://www.unhcr.org/media/wfp-unhcr-guidelines-estimating-food-and-nutritional-needs-emergencies.

30. Interview with Hamdi Said, San Diego, California, April 2019.

31. Interview with Cawo Abdulle, San Diego, California, May 2019.

32. James C. Scott, *Domination and the Arts of Resistance: Hidden Transcripts* (New Haven, CT: Yale University Press, 2009).

33. Interview with Omar Mohamed, San Diego, California, December 2019.

34. Saidiya V. Hartman, *Scenes of Subjection: Terror, Slavery, and Self-Making in Nineteenth-Century America*, 2nd ed. (New York: W.W. Norton, 2022), 7.

35. Hartman, *Scenes of Subjection*, 9.

36. Interview with Omar Mohamed, San Diego, California, December 2019.

37. Scott, *Domination and the Arts of Resistance*, 34.

38. On the ways in which sexuality has been used to deny migrants entry into the United States and the privileging of heteronormative families in family

reunion programs, see Eithne Luibhéid, *Entry Denied: Controlling Sexuality at the Border* (Minneapolis: University of Minnesota Press, 2002).

39. Interview with Safia Mohamed, San Diego, California, April 2019.

40. "Managing Resettlement Effectively," chap. 4, p. 130, in the *UNHCR Resettlement Handbook*, https://www.unhcr.org/us/publications/unhcr-resettlement-handbook-and-country-chapters.

41. Michel Foucault, *The History of Sexuality*, vol. 1, *An Introduction* (New York: Vintage Books, 1990), 95.

42. UNHCR, "Interviewing Applicants for Refugee Status," Training Module RLD4, 1995, chap. 1, https://www.unhcr.org/us/media/training-module-rld4-interviewing-applicants-refugee-status.

43. Aamna Mohdin, "There Are 20 Million Refugees in the World. Less than 1% of Them Have Been Resettled," *Quartz*, May 16, 2016, https://qz.com/685198/there-are-20-million-refugees-in-the-world-less-than-1-of-them-have-been-resettled.

44. "Refugee Act," no. 10 of 2021, sec. 41(1)k, Kenya Law, December 3, 2021, http://kenyalaw.org:8181/exist/kenyalex/actview.xql?actid=No.+10+of+2021.

45. "Juvenile Law (Truancy and Curfew)," Municipal Code 58.0101, 58.0102, and 58.0103, City of San Diego, https://www.sandiego.gov/police/community/juvenile-services/law.

Chapter 3. Confronting Anti-Black Racism

1. Megan Burks, "San Diego's Somali Population: Explained," *Voice of San Diego*, February 22, 2013, https://www.voiceofsandiego.org/community/san-diegos-somali-population-explained/.

2. Office of Immigrant and Refugee Affairs, Health and Human Services Agency, San Diego County, https://www.sandiegocounty.gov/content/sdc/hhsa/programs/sd/community_action_partnership/OfficeofRefugeeCoord.html.

3. Jynnah Radford and Phillip Connor, "Just 10 States Resettled More than Half of Recent Refugees to US," Pew Research Center, December 6, 2016, https://www.pewresearch.org/fact-tank/2016/12/06/just-10-states-resettled-more-than-half-of-recent-refugees-to-u-s/.

4. International Rescue Committee, 2023, https://www.rescue.org/.

5. DroneLab, Qualcomm Institute, University of California, San Diego, http://dronelab.ucsd.edu/.

6. The Somali Family Service, an agency that helps Somalis, dates the first wave of Somali refugee migration to San Diego to 1993.

7. Joe Hughes, "Big Inroads Made in City Heights; Police Reach Out to Young Refugees," *San Diego Union-Tribune*, June 9, 2005, via the Sol Price Center for Social Innovation, University of Sothern California, https://socialinnovation.usc.edu/files/2013/05/Hughes.2005.pdf.

8. *Captain Phillips*, directed by Paul Greengrass, Columbia Pictures, October 2013, https://www.imdb.com/title/tt1535109/.

9. Suzanne Saleeby, "Protectors of the 'Failed State': 'Captain Phillips' and the Intrigue of Somali Pirates," *Jadaliyya*, November 24, 2013, https://www.jadaliyya.com/Details/29853.

10. Min Zhou, "Segmented Assimilation: Issues, Controversies, and Recent Research on the New Second Generation," *International Migration Review* 31, no. 4 (1997): 975–1008.

11. Patrick Moynihan, *The Negro Family: The Case for National Action*, posted on BlackPast website, https://www.blackpast.org/african-american-history/moynihan-report-1965/.

12. See Zhou, "Segmented Assimilation."

13. Interview with Idil Hirsi, San Diego, California, May 2018.

14. Saidiya Hartman, *Lose Your Mother: A Journey along the Atlantic Slave Route* (New York: Farrar, Straus, and Giroux, 2006), 6.

15. Noel Ignatiev, *How the Irish Became White* (London: Routledge, 2015).

16. Stephanie Dickrell, "State Demographer Offers Some Context on Somali Refugee Poverty Numbers," *SC Times*, February 24, 2018, https://www.sctimes.com/story/news/local/immigration/2018/02/24/state-demographer-offers-some-context-somali-refugee-poverty-numbers/370507002/.

17. Randy Capps, Kristen McCabe, and Michael Fix, *Diverse Streams: African Migration to the United States* (Washington, DC: Migration Policy Institute, 2012), 7. https://www.migrationpolicy.org/research/diverse-streams-african-migration-united-states?pdf=africanmigrationus.pdf.

18. Sarah R. Crissey, *Educational Attainment in the United States: 2009* (Washington, DC: US Census Bureau, January 2009). https://shutdown.census.gov/content/dam/Census/library/publications/2012/demo/p20-566.pdf.

19. Interview with Suada Dahir, San Diego, California, November 2020.

20. Matt Furber and Will Wright, "Family Members of Man Killed by Minneapolis Police Say Raid Left Them Shaken," *New York Times*, January 2, 2021, https://www.nytimes.com/2021/01/02/us/minneapolis-police-shooting-raid-dolal-idd.html.

21. Interview with Suada Dahir, San Diego, California, November 2018.

22. Benjamin Aigbe Okonofua, "'I Am Blacker than You': Theorizing Conflict between African Immigrants and African Americans in the United States," *SAGE Open* 3, no. 3 (July–September 2013).

23. Clare Foran, "A Year of Black Lives Matter," *The Atlantic*, December 31, 2015, https://www.theatlantic.com/politics/archive/2015/12/black-lives-matter/421839/.

24. Interview with Jama Ali, San Diego, California, March, 2018.

25. Interview with Hamza Ali, San Diego, California, March 2018.

26. Stuart Hall, "New Ethnicities," in *Stuart Hall: Critical Dialogues in Cultural Studies*, eds. David Morley and Kuan-Hsing Chen (London: Routledge, 1996), 442.

27. Hughes, "Big Inroads Made in City Heights."

28. The SDPD website provides a detailed description of curfew laws. See "Juvenile Law (Truancy and Curfew)," Municipal Code 58.0101, 58.0102, and 58.0103, City of San Deigo website, https://www.sandiego.gov/police/community/juvenile-services/law.

29. Interview with Nasir Ahmed, San Diego, California, March 2018.

30. Katie Hyson, "Curfews Don't Work, but San Diego Police Still Enforce Them—Mostly for Black and Latino Youth," KPBS news, September 8, 2023, https://www.kpbs.org/news/racial-justice-social-equity/2023/09/08/curfews-dont-work-but-san-diego-police-still-enforce-them-mostly-for-black-and-latino-youth.

31. Interview with Safia Abdullahi, San Diego, California, May 2019.

32. Frank B. Wilderson III, "'We're Trying to Destroy the World': Anti-Blackness & Police Violence after Ferguson," interview by Jared Ball, Todd Steven Burroughs, and Dr. Hate, Imixwhatilike.org, recorded October 1, 2014, https://imixwhatilike.org/2014/10/01/frankwildersonandantiblackness-2/.

33. Dorothy E. Roberts, "Race, Vagueness, and the Social Meaning of Order-Maintenance Policing," *Journal of Criminal Law & Criminology* 89, no. 3 (Spring 1999): 806.

34. "Violent Crime Control and Law Enforcement Act of 1994," H.R. 3355, 103rd Congress (1993–94), https://www.congress.gov/bill/103rd-congress/house-bill/3355.

35. US Department of Justice, "Investigation of the Chicago Police Department," January 13, 2017, p. 5, Office of Public Affairs, US Department of Justice, via the "Chicago Police Department Findings," https://www.justice.gov/opa/pr/justice-department-announces-findings-investigation-chicago-police-department.

36. David W. McIvor, "Black Lives Matter and the Democratic Work of Mourning," in *Mourning in America: Race and the Politics of Loss* (Ithaca, NY: Cornell University Press, 2016), 161–84.

37. Interview with Yasmin Omar, San Diego, California, April 2018.

38. Saidiya V. Hartman, *Scenes of Subjection Terror, Slavery, and Self-Making in Nineteenth-Century America*, 2nd ed. (New York: W. W. Norton, 2022).

39. Barbara Ransby, *Making All Black Lives Matter: Reimagining Freedom in the Twenty-First Century* (Oakland: University of California Press, 2018), 73.

40. Interview with Aisha Ahmed, San Diego, California, June 2019.

41. Furber and Wright, "Family Members of Man Killed by Minneapolis Police Say Raid Left Them Shaken."

42. Interview with Abdikareem Mire, San Diego, California, June 2017.

43. Khalil Gibran Muhammad, *The Condemnation of Blackness: Race, Crime, and the Making of Modern Urban America* (Cambridge, MA: Harvard University Press, 2019).

44. Frantz Fanon, *Black Skin, White Masks*, new ed., trans. Richard Philcox (New York: Grove Press, 2008), 93.

45. Interview with Ilyas Idle, San Diego, California, June 2018.

46. Ashley D. Farmer, *Remaking Black Power: How Black Women Transformed an Era* (Chapel Hill: University of North Carolina Press, 2019), 56.

47. David Garrick, "Gloria Proposes More Scrutiny, Restrictions on San Diego Police Use of Military Weapons," *San Diego Union-Tribune*, August 28, 2021. https://www.sandiegouniontribune.com/news/politics/story/2021-08-28/gloria-proposing-greater-scrutiny-restrictions-on-use-of-military-weapons-by.

48. Simone Browne, *Dark Matters: On the Surveillance of Blackness* (Durham, NC: Duke University Press, 2015), 34.

49. Interview with Mohamed Warsame, San Diego, California, September 2019.

50. Mari Payton, Dorian Hargrove, Tom Jones, and Jay Yoo, "La Mesa Police Release Timeline of May 30 Demonstration," NBC 7 San Diego, June 9, 2020. https://www.nbcsandiego.com/news/investigations/la-mesa-police-release-timeline-of-may-30-demonstration/2343500/.

51. Cheryl I. Harris, "Whiteness as Property," *Harvard Law Review* 106, no. 8 (1993): 1714.

52. George Lipsitz, "The Possessive Investment in Whiteness: Racialized Social Democracy and the 'White' Problem in American Studies," *American Quarterly* 47, no. 3 (1995): 372.

53. Saunders quoted in May Tjoa, "NBC 7 Exclusive: Inside San Diego Police Department SWAT Training," NBC 7 San Diego, February 15, 2015, https://www.nbcsandiego.com/news/local/san-diegos-swat-unit-marks-30th-anniversary/84015/.

54. San Diego Tourism Authority, "Military Information: From Bases to the USO to Public Affairs Offices," 2023, https://www.sandiego.org/articles/military/military-information.aspx.

55. Quoted in Tjoa, "NBC 7 Exclusive: Inside San Diego Police Department SWAT Training."

56. Council on Criminal Justice, "No-Knock Warrants and Police Raids," Task Force on Policing, policy assessment, January 2021, p. 2, https://counciloncj.foleon.com/policing/assessing-the-evidence/iii-no-knock-warrants-and-police-raids.

57. Radley Balko, *Rise of the Warrior Cop: The Militarization of America's Police Forces* (New York: Public Affairs, 2021).

58. Interview with Tahim Barre, San Diego, California, June 2019.

59. Megan Burks, "The Fine Line between Gang Policing and Gang Behavior," Voice of San Diego, March 3, 2014, https://voiceofsandiego.org/2014/03/03/the-fine-line-between-gang-policing-and-gang-behavior/.

60. Jonathan Mummolo, "Militarization Fails to Enhance Police Safety or Reduce Crime but May Harm Police Reputation," *PNAS* 115, no. 37 (September 2018).

61. Interview with Barsanji Ahmed, California, September 2019.

62. Interview with Ayaan Yusuf, San Diego, California, November 2019.

63. Interview with Barsanji Ahmed, San Diego, California, September 2019.

64. Interview with Liban Aden, San Diego, California, September 2018.

65. Interview with Ahmed Abdullahi, San Diego, California, May 2017. According to the *Uniform Crime Report* by the FBI, Black youths are uniformly targeted for arrests. See Federal Bureau of Investigation, "Crime in the United States, 2013," FBI *Uniform Crime Report*, 2013, https://ucr.fbi.gov/crime-in-the-u.s/2013/crime-in-the-u.s.-2013.

66. Interview with Zach Yusuf, San Diego, California, October 2020.

67. Interview with Ali Maxamed, San Diego, California, May 2019.

68. Kim Crockett, "Is Welfare Fraud Funding Al-Shabaab?" *Thinking Minnesota*, no. 12 (Summer 2018), Center of the American Experiment, https://www.americanexperiment.org/magazine/article/is-welfare-fraud-funding-al-shabaab.

69. Campaign Zero, *Evaluating Policing in San Diego*, ACLU of San Diego report, 2019, p. 4, https://www.sandiegocounty.gov/content/dam/sdc/clerb/docs/disparities-in-local-policing/1121AttachI-DisparitiesInLocalPolicing.pdf.

70. Interview with Abdikareem Gure, San Diego, California, January 2019.

71. See Emma Pierson et al., "A Large-Scale Analysis of Racial Disparities in Police Stops across the United States," *Nature Human Behaviour* 4 (July 2020): 736–45.

72. Interview with Abdikareem Gure, San Diego, California, January 2019.

73. Interview with Faysal Hassan, San Diego, California, January 2019.

74. "Attorney General's Annual Report on Calgang for 2019," State of California Department of Justice, https://oag.ca.gov/calgang/reports.

75. Cody Dulaney, "'Seize the Time': San Diego Activists Join Call to Stop Labeling People as Gang Members," inewsource, June 30, 2020, https://inewsource.org/2020/06/30/california-gang-database-calgang/.

76. On how gang databases are used as a tool of racial profiling, see Dana Littlefield, "San Diego Lawmaker Wants More Transparency in Gang Database," *San Diego Union-Tribune*, November 5, 2016, https://www.sandiegouniontribune.com/news/courts/sd-me-gang-audit-20161025-story.html.

77. SB 458: Gangs: Statewide Database, California legislative session 2013–14, bill passed October 13, 2013, https://legiscan.com/CA/text/SB458/id/866815.

78. Dulaney, "'Seize the Time.'"

79. Victor M. Rios, *Punished: Policing the Lives of Black and Latino Boys* (New York: NYU Press, 2011), 78.

80. Interview with Abdirahim Hassan, San Diego, California, January 2019.

81. Browne, *Dark Matters*, 8.

82. Interview with Cumar Faraax, San Diego, California, September 2020.

83. San Diego crime map, Crime Mapping, https://www.crimemapping.com/map/location/San%20Diego.

84. Police Executive Research Forum, *Critical Response Technical Assessment Review: Police Accountability—Findings and National Implications of an Assessment of the San Diego Police Department* (Washington, DC: Office of Community Oriented Policing Services, 2015), https://portal.cops.usdoj.gov/resourcecenter/Home.aspx?page=detail&id=COPS-W0756.

85. Camilla Hawthorne and Jovan Scott Lewis, "Black Geographies: Material Praxis of Black Life and Study," in *The Black Geographic: Praxis, Resistance, Futurity*, eds. Camila Hawthorne and Jovan Scott Lewis (Durham, NC: Duke University Press, 2023), 7.

86. Interview with Jamal Hussein, San Diego, California, April 2017.

87. Katherine McKittrick, *Demonic Grounds: Black Women and the Cartographies of Struggle* (Minneapolis: University of Minnesota Press, 2006), 21–22.

88. Interview with Omar Muse, San Diego, California, April 2017.

89. Kevin Loria, "Military Veterans to Get Priority for Police Jobs under COPS Grants," *Christian Science Monitor*, June 25, 2012, https://www.csmonitor.com/USA/2012/0625/Military-veterans-to-get-priority-for-police-jobs-under-COPS-grants.

90. For a discussion of use of force, see "San Diego Sheriff's Department Policies and Procedures," San Diego Sheriff's Department, last updated May 17, 2023, https://www.sdsheriff.gov/bureaus/about-us/policies-procedures.

91. Interview with Eidle Ali, San Diego, California, February 2017.

92. Interview with Eidle Ali, San Diego, California, February 2017.

93. Arthur Rizer and Joseph Hartman, "How the War on Terror Has Militarized the Police," *The Atlantic*, November 7, 2017, https://www.theatlantic.com/national/archive/2011/11/how-the-war-on-terror-has-militarized-the-police/248047/.

Chapter 4. Somali Refugees and the War on Terror

1. Kelly Thornton, "Three Indicted in Political Asylum Case," *San Diego Union-Tribune*, June 29, 2003, https://www.sandiegouniontribune.com/sdut-three-indicted-political-asylum-case-2003jun29-story.html.

2. Interview with Axlam Mahat, San Diego, California, May 2019.

3. Interview with Faysal Said, San Diego, California, June 2018.

4. Andrew G. Mills and Joseph R. Clark, "Running a Three-Legged Race: The San Diego Police Department, the Intelligence Community, and Counterterrorism," Homeland Security Policy Institute, George Washington University, brief 12, August 1, 2011, p. 13, https://www.jstor.org/stable/resrep20744.

5. Interview with Aamiina Xasan, San Diego, California, June 2018.

6. Henry Giroux, *The University in Chains: Confronting the Military-Industrial-Academic Complex* (Abingdon: Routledge, 2016), 39.

7. *United States of America v. Mohamed Abdihamid Farah (02), Abdirahman Yasin Daud (04), and Guled Ali Omar (07)*, US District Court of Minnesota, May 9, 2016.

8. Ma Vang, *History on the Run: Secrecy, Fugitivity, and Hmong Refugee Epistemologies* (Durham, NC: Duke University Press, 2021), 7.

9. Interview with Axado Hussein, San Diego, California, May 2018.

10. National Defense Authorization Act for Fiscal Year 2012, https://www.congress.gov/112/plaws/publ81/PLAW-112publ81.pdf.

11. Interview with Ifrah Hussein, San Diego, California, April 2017.

12. Besheer Mohamed and Jeff Diamant, "Black Muslims Account for a Fifth of All US Muslims, and about Half Are Converts to Islam," Pew Research Center, January 17, 2019, https://www.pewresearch.org/fact-tank/2019/01/17/black-muslims-account-for-a-fifth-of-all-u-s-muslims-and-about-half-are-converts-to-islam/.

13. Interview with Khalif Mohamed, San Diego, California, April 2017.

14. Su'ad Abdul Khabeer, *Muslim Cool: Race, Religion, and Hip Hop in the United States* (New York: NYU Press, 2016), 69.

15. *Muslim Americans: No Signs of Growth in Alienation or Support for Extremism*, Pew Research Center, August 30, 2011, https://www.pewresearch.org/politics/2011/08/30/muslim-americans-no-signs-of-growth-in-alienation-or-support-for-extremism/.

16. Andrea Huncar, "Mustafa Mattan Shot Dead through Fort McMurray Apartment Door," CBC News, February 12, 2015, https://www.cbc.ca/news/canada/edmonton/mustafa-mattan-shot-dead-through-fort-mcmurray-apartment-door-1.2954439.

17. Khaled A. Beydoun and Margari Hill, "The Colour of Muslim Mourning," Al Jazeera, February 15, 2015, https://www.aljazeera.com/opinions/2015/2/15/the-colour-of-muslim-mourning.

18. Interview with Mohamed Gedi, San Diego, California, April 2017.

19. For the aftermath of the shooting, see Don Crothers, "Abdi Mohamed: Teen Shot by Salt Lake City Police Awakens from Coma," *Inquisitr*, May 13, 2016, https://www.inquisitr.com/2886331/abdi-mohamed-awakens-from-coma/.

20. Interview by Sahal Jama, San Diego, California, April 2017.

21. Interview with Yasmin Nur, San Diego, California, April 2018.

22. Basima Sisemore and Elsadig Elsheikh, "The Pervasiveness of Islamophobia in the United States," Othering & Belonging Institute, University of California, Berkeley, July 21, 2022, https://belonging.berkeley.edu/pervasiveness-islamophobia-united-states.

23. Randy Borum, "Radicalization into Violent Extremism II: A Review of Conceptual Models and Empirical Research," *Journal of Strategic Security* 4, no. 4 (2011): 37–62. https://doi.org/10.5038/1944-0472.4.4.2.

24. Marieke Slootman and Jean Tillie, *Processes of Radicalisation: Why Some Amsterdam Muslims become Radicals* (Amsterdam: Institute for Migration and Ethnic Studies, 2006).

25. Graeme R. Newman and Ronald V. Clarke, *Policing Terrorism: An Executive's Guide* (Washington, DC: Office of Community Oriented Policing Services, US Department of Justice, 2008), 16.

26. Mills and Clark, "Running a Three-Legged Race."

27. Special Investigations Division, San Diego County Sheriff's Department, 2023, https://www.sdsheriff.gov/bureaus/law-enforcement-services-bureau/support-services/special-investigations-division.

28. Somali Family Service, "Programs: Economic Development, Microenterprise Program," 2023, https://www.somalifamilyservice.org/index.php/programs/economic-development.html.

29. Simone Browne, *Dark Matters: On the Surveillance of Blackness* (Durham, NC: Duke University Press, 2015), 68.

30. See Office of Juvenile Justice and Delinquency Prevention's National Gang Center, *OJJDP Comprehensive Gang Model: Planning for Implementation*, 2009, https://www.nationalgangcenter.gov/Content/Documents/Implementation-Manual/Implementation-Manual.pdf

31. See Office of Juvenile Justice and Delinquency Prevention's National Gang Center, *OJJDP Comprehensive Gang Model: Planning for Implementation*.

32. "San Diego ACLU Concerned about FBI Surveillance of Somali Community," ACLU of San Diego and Imperial Counties, June 1, 2011, https://www.aclu-sdic.org/en/news/san-diego-aclu-concerned-about-fbi-surveillance-somali-community.

33. Interview with Caaisho Nur, San Diego, California, January 2018.

34. Uniting and Strengthening America by Providing Appropriate Tools Required to Intercept and Obstruct Terrorism Act (USA Patriot Act), 2001, section 205.

35. "Harbor Police Special Units and Task Forces," Port Authority of San Diego, https://www.portofsandiego.org/public-safety/harbor-police/special-units-and-task-forces.

36. American Civil Liberties Union, *War Comes Home: The Excessive Militarization of American Policing* (New York: ACLU, 2014), 2, https://www.aclu.org/sites/default/files/assets/jus14-warcomeshome-report-web-rel1.pdf.

37. Mills and Clark, "Running a Three-Legged Race," 3.

38. "US Census Bureau Quickfacts: San Diego City, California," US Census Bureau, 2022, https://www.census.gov/quickfacts/fact/table/sandiegocitycalifornia/PST045222. For data on the Somali population, see Somali Family Service, "Programs: Economic Development, Microenterprise Program."

39. Interview with Abdiraxman Sayid, San Diego, California, September 2019.

40. See Stuart Hall et al., *Policing the Crisis: Mugging, the State and Law and Order*, 2nd ed. (London: Macmillan, 2013).

41. Interview with Hashim Nur, San Diego, California, October 2018.

42. Interview with Bishaaro Fasal, San Diego, California, March 2018.

43. Spencer Ackerman, "FBI Teaches Agents: 'Mainstream' Muslims Are 'Violent, Radical,'" *Wired*, September 14, 2011, https://www.wired.com/2011/09/fbi-muslims-radical/.

44. Interview with Bishaaro Fasal, San Diego, California, March 2018.

45. "Legacy of the 'Dark Side': The Costs of Unlawful US Detentions and Interrogations Post-9/11," Human Rights Watch, January 9, 2022, https://www.hrw.org/news/2022/01/09/legacy-dark-side. See also Jeremy Scahill, "The CIA's Secret Sites in Somalia," *The Nation*, December 10, 2014, https://www.thenation.com/article/archive/cias-secret-sites-somalia/.

46. Interview with Maxamed Farah, San Diego, California, November 2018.

47. "The Third Jihad: Radical Islam's Vision for America," *Haaretz*, August 13, 2009, https://www.haaretz.com/2009-08-13/ty-article/the-third-jihad-radical-islams-vision-for-america/0000017f-e564-dea7-adff-f5ffe2560000.

48. Michael Powell, "In Police Training, a Dark Film on US Muslims," *New York Times*, January 23, 2012, https://www.nytimes.com/2012/01/24/nyregion/in-police-training-a-dark-film-on-us-muslims.html.

49. *The Third Jihad: Radical Islam's Vision for America*, directed by Wayne Kopping, Clarion Project, 2008, https://clarionproject.org/films/third-jihad/.

50. Ayaan Hirsi Ali, *Infidel: My Life* (London: Pocket Books, 2008), 38.

51. "NYCLU Statement on NYPD Deceit over 'Third Jihad' Movie," New York Civil Liberties Union, February 1, 2012, https://www.nyclu.org/en/press-releases/nyclu-statement-nypd-deceit-over-third-jihad-movie.

52. Anthony Bogues, *Empire of Liberty: Power, Desire & Freedom* (Lebanon, NH: University Press of New England, 2010).

53. Fatima El-Tayeb, "Time Travelers and Queer Heterotopia: Narratives from the Muslim Underground," *Germanic Review: Literature, Culture, Theory* 88, no. 3 (2013): 36.

54. Samuel P. Huntington, *The Clash of Civilizations and the Remaking of World Order* (London: Penguin, 2014).

55. Mahmood Mamdani, *Good Muslim, Bad Muslim: America, The Cold War, and the Roots of Terror* (Lagos: Malthouse Press, 2006), 33

56. Amnesty International, *The Hidden US War in Somalia: Civilian Casualties from Air Strikes in Lower Shabelle* (London: Amnesty International, 2019), 26, https://www.amnesty.org/en/documents/afr52/9952/2019/en/.

57. Hamza Mohamed, "A Family Mourns as US Drone Attacks in Somalia Continue," Al Jazeera, April 1, 2020, https://www.aljazeera.com/features/2020/4/1/a-family-mourns-as-us-drone-attacks-in-somalia-continue.

58. Amnesty International, *The Hidden US War*, 30.

59. Jeremy Scahill, *Dirty Wars: The World Is a Battlefield* (London: Serpent's Tale, 2014), 56.

60. Interview with Abdirazak Mohamed, San Diego, California, June 2018.

61. Neta C. Crawford, *Human Cost of the Post-9/11 Wars: Lethality and the Need for Transparency*, report (Providence, RI: Watson Institute of International and Public Affairs, Brown University, November 2018), 2–3, https://

watson.brown.edu/costsofwar/papers/2018/human-cost-post-911-wars-lethality-and-need-transparency.

62. Jack Serle, "Does al Shabaab Strike Signal Change in US Tactics in Somalia?" Bureau of Investigative Journalism, February 6, 2015, https://www.thebureauinvestigates.com/stories/2015-02-06/does-latest-drone-strike-on-al-shabaab-signal-change-in-us-tactics-in-somalia.

63. Jack Serle, "Unprecedented Death Toll from US Air Strike in Somalia," Bureau of Investigative Journalism, May 7, 2016, https://www.thebureauinvestigates.com/stories/2016-03-07/unprecedented-death-toll-from-us-air-strike-in-somalia.

64. *US Africa Command Civilian Casualty Assessment Quarterly Report*, 2nd quarter, FY2020, United States Africa Command, https://www.africom.mil/us-africa-command-civilian-casualty-assessment-quarterly-report-2nd-quarter-fy2020.

65. Interview with Hawa Hussein, San Diego, California, April 2018.

66. Amnesty International, *The Hidden US War*, 34.

67. Interview with Hawa Hussein, San Diego, California, April 2018.

68. *US Africa Command Civilian Casualty Assessment Quarterly Report*.

69. Interview with Hawa Hussein, San Diego, California, April 2018.

70. Elliot Spagat, "US Citizen Raised in San Diego Faces New Terrorism Charges," *San Diego Union-Tribune*, December 2, 2019, https://www.sandiegouniontribune.com/news/california/story/2019-12-02/new-terrorism-indictment-for-us-man-linked-to-somali-group.

71. Interview with Nimo Mohamed, San Diego, California, April 2019.

72. Ty McCormick, "US Operates Drones from Secret Bases in Somalia," *Foreign Policy*, July 2, 2015, https://foreignpolicy.com/2015/07/02/exclusive-u-s-operates-drones-from-secret-bases-in-somalia-special-operations-jsoc-black-hawk-down/.

73. Interview with Abdinasir Hussein, San Diego, California, October 2018.

74. Nick Turse, "Pentagon's Own Map of US Bases in Africa Contradicts Its Claim of 'Light' Footprint," *The Intercept*, February 27, 2020, https://theintercept.com/2020/02/27/africa-us-military-bases-africom/.

75. Interview with Caaliyah Hussein, San Diego, California, June 2018.

76. Amnesty International, *The Hidden US War*, 8.

77. Interview with Ifrah Hassan, San Diego, California, April 2019.

78. "Al Shabaab's American Recruits," Anti-Defamation League, February 24, 2015, https://www.adl.org/news/article/al-shabaabs-american-recruits.

79. Clemens Greiner and Patrick Sakdapolrak argue that "translocality is used to describe socio-spatial dynamics and processes of simultaneity and identity formation that transcend boundaries—including, but also extending beyond, those of nation states." Grenier and Sakdapolrak, "Translocality: Concepts, Applications and Emerging Research Perspectives," *Geography Compass* 7, no. 5 (2013): 373.

80. Interview with Abucar Guled, San Diego, California, April 2019.

81. "'There Are No Expendable American Targets,'" President Bill Clinton's statement from the Oval Office, Federal Documents Clearing House, August 21, 1998, https://www.washingtonpost.com/wp-srv/inatl/longterm/eafricabombing/stories/text082098b.htm.

82. Refugee Processing Center archives, 2023, https://www.wrapsnet.org/archives/. Data can also be found in David Bier, "Trump Cut Muslim Refugees 91%, Immigrants 30%, Visitors by 18%," Cato at Liberty (blog), Cato Institute, December 7, 2018, https://www.cato.org/blog/trump-cut-muslim-refugees-91-immigrants-30-visitors-18.

83. "Somalia Population 2023 (Live)," World Population Review, https://worldpopulationreview.com/countries/Somalia-population.

Conclusion

1. Evan Hill, Ainara Tiefenthäler, Christiaan Triebert, Drew Jordan, Haley Willis, and Robin Stein, "How George Floyd Was Killed in Police Custody," *New York Times*, June 1, 2020, https://www.nytimes.com/2020/05/31/us/george-floyd-investigation.html.

2. Interview with Amina Nur, San Diego, California, November 2020.

3. "Somali Population," Minnesota Compass, 2023, https://www.mncompass.org/topics/demographics/cultural-communities/somali.

4. Hibah Ansari, "A Quiet Storm: Unraveling the Kind Heart, Troubled Mind, and Sudden Death of Dolal Idd," *Sahan Journal*, March 22, 2021, https://sahanjournal.com/policing-justice/family-dolal-idd-killing-minneapolis-police/.

5. "Crime in the US 2019," FBI Uniform Crime Reporting, https://ucr.fbi.gov/crime-in-the-u.s/2019/crime-in-the-u.s.-2019.

6. Interview with Yasmin Farah, San Diego, California, December 2020.

7. Robin D.G. Kelley, *Freedom Dreams: The Black Radical Imagination* (Boston: Beacon Press, 2002).

8. "Police Violence against Black People Is on the Rise in Brazil," *GIGA Focus*, no. 5 (2020), https://www.giga-hamburg.de/en/publications/giga-focus/police-violence-against-black-people-is-on-the-rise-in-brazil.

9. Interview with Aisha Mohamed, San Diego, California, November 2020.

10. Reema Ghabra, "Black Immigrants Face Unique Challenges," Human Rights First (blog), February 17, 2022, https://humanrightsfirst.org/library/black-immigrants-face-unique-challenges/.

11. Rinaldo Walcott, *The Long Emancipation: Moving toward Black Freedom* (Durham, NC: Duke University Press, 2021), 31.

12. Yến Lê Espiritu, *Body Counts: The Vietnam War and Militarized Refuge(es)* (Oakland, CA: University of California Press, 2014); Long T. Bui, *Returns of War: South Vietnam and the Price of Refugee Memory* (New York: NYU Press, 2018); Simeon Man, *Soldiering through Empire: Race and the Making of the Decolonizing Pacific* (Oakland: University of California Press, 2018).

13. Ruth Wilson Gilmore, *Golden Gulag: Prisons, Surplus, Crisis, and Opposition in Globalizing California* (Berkeley: University of California Press, 2007); Khalil Gibran Muhammad, *The Condemnation of Blackness: Race, Crime, and the Making of Modern Urban America* (Cambridge, MA: Harvard University Press, 2019); Angela Y. Davis, *Are Prisons Obsolete?* (New York: Seven Stories Press, 2011); Joy James, *Resisting State Violence: Radicalism, Gender, and Race in US Culture* (Minneapolis: University of Minnesota Press, 1997).

14. Interview with Fahima Hassan, San Diego, California, November 2020.

15. Nick Turse, "Pentagon's Own Map of US Bases in Africa Contradicts Its Claim of 'Light' Footprint," *The Intercept*, February 27, 2020, https://theintercept.com/2020/02/27/africa-us-military-bases-africom/.

16. Interview with Ahmed Ali, San Diego, California, October 2020.

17. Mariame Kaba and Andrea J. Ritchie, *No More Police: A Case for Abolition* (New York: The New Press, 2022), 11.

18. Andrew G. Mills and Joseph R. Clark, "Running a Three-Legged Race: The San Diego Police Department, the Intelligence Community, and

Counterterrorism," Homeland Security Policy Institute, George Washington University, HSPI brief 12, August 1, 2011, https://www.jstor.org/stable/resrep20744.

19. Stuart Schrader, *Badges without Borders: How Global Counterinsurgency Transformed American Policing* (Oakland: University of California Press, 2019), 45.

20. Schrader, *Badges without Borders*, 80.

21. Mukhtar M. Ibrahim, "Transit Police Chief Harrington Pays Visit to Somalia," MPR News, July 30, 2015, https://www.mprnews.org/story/2015/07/30/transit-police-chief-harrington-pays-visit-to-somalia.

22. Shawn Musgrave, Tom Meagher, and Gabriel Dance, "The Pentagon Finally Details Its Weapons-for-Cops Giveaway: Bellying Up to the Arsenal," The Marshall Project, December 4, 2014, https://www.themarshallproject.org/2014/12/03/the-pentagon-finally-details-its-weapons-for-cops-giveaway.

23. "Al-Shabaab in East Africa: 2004–2022," timeline, Council on Foreign Relations, 2022, https://www.cfr.org/timeline/al-shabaab-east-africa.

24. Osman Osman, "Kenyan Somali Refugees Claim They Are Denied Citizenship Rights," Al Jazeera, May 19, 2019, https://www.aljazeera.com/features/2019/5/19/kenyan-somali-refugees-claim-they-are-denied-citizenship-rights.

25. Amelia Cheatham and Diana Roy, "US Detention of Child Migrants," Council on Foreign Relations, updated March 27, 2023, https://www.cfr.org/backgrounder/us-detention-child-migrants.

26. "Scandal over Kenya's Border Fence That Cost $35m for Just 10km," BBC News, March 14, 2019, https://www.bbc.com/news/world-africa-47574463.

27. Michelle Mark, "Trump Just Referred to One of His Most Infamous Campaign Comments: Calling Mexicans 'Rapists,'" *Business Insider*, April 5, 2018, https://www.businessinsider.com/trump-mexicans-rapists-remark-reference-2018-4.

28. Michelle Alexander, *The New Jim Crow: Mass Incarceration in the Age of Colorblindness* (New York: The New Press, 2020).

29. Treva B. Lindsey, *America, Goddam: Violence, Black Women, and the Struggle for Justice* (Oakland: University of California Press, 2023), 80–81.

30. Interview with Aisha Mohamed, San Diego, California, November 2020.

Bibliography

Abdi, Cawo M. "Convergence of Civil War and the Religious Right: Reimagining Somali Women." *Signs: Journal of Women in Culture and Society* 33, no. 1 (2007): 183–207.

———. *Elusive Jannah: The Somali Diaspora and a Borderless Muslim Identity.* Minneapolis: University of Minnesota Press, 2015.

Abuhakema, Ghazi, and Tim Carmichael. "The Somali Youth League Constitution: A Handwritten Arabic Copy (c. 1947?) from the Ethiopian Security Forces Archives in Harär." *Journal of Eastern African Studies* 4, no. 3 (2010): 450–66.

Aidid, Safia. "*Haweenku Wa Garab* (Women Are a Force): Women and the Somali Nationalist Movement, 1943–1960." *Bildhaan: An International Journal of Somali Studies* 10 (2010): 103–24.

Alexander, Michelle. *The New Jim Crow: Mass Incarceration in the Age of Colorblindness.* New York: The New Press, 2020.

Ali, Ayaan Hirsi. *Infidel: My Life.* London: Pocket Books, 2008.

American Civil Liberties Union. *War Comes Home: The Excessive Militarization of American Policing.* New York: ACLU, 2014. https://www.aclu.org/sites/default/files/assets/jus14-warcomeshome-report-web-rel1.pdf.

Amnesty International. *Annual Report 1989.* London: Amnesty International Publications, 1989. https://www.amnesty.org/en/documents/pol10/0002/1989/en/.

———. *The Hidden US War in Somalia: Civilian Casualties from Air Strikes in Lower Shabelle.* London: Amnesty International, 2019. https://www.amnesty.org/en/documents/afr52/9952/2019/en/.

Anderson, Monica. "African Immigrant Population in US Steadily Climbs." Pew Research Center. February 14, 2017. https://www.pewresearch.org/fact-tank/2017/02/14/african-immigrant-population-in-u-s-steadily-climbs/.

Atanasoski, Neda. *Humanitarian Violence: The US Deployment of Diversity.* Minneapolis: University of Minnesota Press, 2013.

Attorney General's Annual Report on Calgang for 2019. State of California Department of Justice. https://oag.ca.gov/calgang/reports.

Auston, Donna. "Prayer, Protest, and Police Brutality: Black Muslim Spiritual Resistance in the Ferguson Era." *Transforming Anthropology* 25, no. 1 (2017): 11–22.

Balko, Radley. *Rise of the Warrior Cop: The Militarization of America's Police Forces.* 2nd ed. New York: Public Affairs, 2021. Kindle edition.

Besteman, Catherine Lowe. *Making Refuge: Somali Bantu Refugees and Lewiston, Maine.* Durham, NC: Duke University Press, 2016.

Bogues, Anthony. *Empire of Liberty: Power, Desire & Freedom.* Lebanon, NH: University Press of New England, 2010. Kindle edition.

Borgen, Linda, and Rubén Rumbaut. "Coming of Age in 'America's Finest City': Transitions to Adulthood among Children of Immigrants in San Diego." In *Coming of Age in America*, eds. Mary C. Waters, Patrick J. Carr, Maria J. Kefalas, and Jennifer Holdaway, 133–68. Berkeley: University of California Press, 2011.

Borum, Randy. "Radicalization into Violent Extremism II: A Review of Conceptual Models and Empirical Research." *Journal of Strategic Security* 4, no. 4 (2011): 37–62.

Boutros-Ghali, Boutros. *The United Nations and Somalia, 1992–1996.* New York: United Nations Department of Public Information, 1996.

Browne, Simone. *Dark Matters: On the Surveillance of Blackness.* Durham, NC: Duke University Press, 2015.

Bui, Long T. "The Refugee Repertoire: Performing and Staging the Postmemories of Violence." *MELUS* 41, no. 3 (2016): 112–32.

———. *Returns of War: South Vietnam and the Price of Refugee Memory.* New York: NYU Press, 2018.

Campaign Zero. *Evaluating Policing in San Diego.* San Diego: ACLU of San Diego, 2019. https://www.sandiegocounty.gov/content/dam/sdc/clerb/docs/disparities-in-local-policing/1121AttachI-DisparitiesInLocalPolicing.pdf.

Capps, Randy, Kristen McCabe, and Michael Fix. *Diverse Streams: African Migration to the United States*. Washington, DC: Migration Policy Institute, 2012. https://www.migrationpolicy.org/research/diverse-streams-african-migration-united-states?pdf=africanmigrationus.pdf.

Cheatham, Amelia, and Diana Roy. "US Detention of Child Migrants." Council on Foreign Relations. Updated March 27, 2023. https://www.cfr.org/backgrounder/us-detention-child-migrants.

Cohen, Bernard C. "A View from the Academy." In *Taken by Storm: The Media, Public Opinion, and US Foreign Policy in the Gulf War*, eds. W. Lance Bennett and David L. Paletz, 8–11. Chicago: University of Chicago Press, 1994.

Council on Criminal Justice. "No-Knock Warrants and Police Raids." Task Force on Policing. Policy assessment, January 2021. https://counciloncj.foleon.com/policing/assessing-the-evidence/iii-no-knock-warrants-and-police-raids.

Crawford, Neta C. *Human Cost of the Post-9/11 Wars: Lethality and the Need for Transparency*. Research paper. Providence, RI: Watson Institute of International & Public Affairs, Brown University, November 2018. https://watson.brown.edu/costsofwar/papers/2018/human-cost-post-911-wars-lethality-and-need-transparency.

Crissey, Sarah R. *Educational Attainment in the United States: 2009*. Washington, DC: US Census Bureau, January 2009. https://shutdown.census.gov/content/dam/Census/library/publications/2012/demo/p20-566.pdf.

Curtis, Edward E. "African-American Islamization Reconsidered: Black History Narratives and Muslim Identity." *Journal of the American Academy of Religion* 73, no. 3 (2005): 659–84.

Davis, Angela Y. *Are Prisons Obsolete?* New York: Seven Stories Press, 2011.

Davis, Muriam Haleh. "'Incommensurate Ontologies'? Anti-Black Racism and the Question of Islam in French Algeria." *Lateral* 10, no. 1 (2021).

DeSilver, Drew. "How the US Compares with Other Countries Taking in Refugees." Pew Research Center, September 24, 2015. https://www.pewresearch.org/fact-tank/2015/09/24/how-the-u-s-compares-with-other-countries-taking-in-refugees/.

Dudziak, Mary L. *Cold War Civil Rights: Race and the Image of American Democracy*. Princeton, NJ: Princeton University Press, 2011.

El-Tayeb, Fatima. "Time Travelers and Queer Heterotopia: Narratives from the Muslim Underground." *The Germanic Review: Literature, Culture, Theory* 88, no. 3 (2013): 305–19.

Eshete, Tibebe. "Towards a History of the Incorporation of the Ogaden: 1887–1935." *Journal of Ethiopian Studies* 27, no. 2 (1994): 69–87.

Espiritu, Yến Lê. *Body Counts: The Vietnam War and Militarized Refuge(es)*. Oakland: University of California Press, 2014.

Fanon, Frantz. *Black Skin, White Masks*. New edition. Translated by Richard Philcox. New York: Grove Press, 2008.

Farmer, Ashley D. *Remaking Black Power: How Black Women Transformed an Era*. Chapel Hill: University of North Carolina Press, 2019.

Federal Bureau of Investigation. *Crime in the United States, 2013*. FBI Uniform Crime Report, 2013. https://ucr.fbi.gov/crime-in-the-u.s/2013/crime-in-the-u.s.-2013.

Fedirka, Allison. "Why the US Cares about Somalia." Geopolitical Futures, May 10, 2017. https://geopoliticalfutures.com/us-cares-somalia/.

Ferguson, Roderick A. "The Lateral Moves of African American Studies in a Period of Migration." In *Strange Affinities: The Gender and Sexual Politics of Comparative Racialization*, eds. Grace Kyungwon Hong and Roderick A. Ferguson, 113–30. Durham, NC: Duke University Press, 2011.

Foucault, Michel. *The History of Sexuality*. Vol. 1: *An Introduction*. New York: Vintage Books, 1990.

Gawthrop, Elisabeth. "The Color of Coronavirus: Covid-19 Deaths Analyzed by Race and Ethnicity in the US." Color of Coronavirus Project: Key Findings. APM Research Lab. October 19, 2023. https://www.apmresearchlab.org/covid/deaths-by-race.

Gilkes, Patrick. "Somalia: Conflicts within and against the Military Regime." *Review of African Political Economy* 16, no. 44 (1989): 53–58.

Gilmore, Ruth Wilson. *Golden Gulag: Prisons, Surplus, Crisis, and Opposition in Globalizing California*. Berkeley: University of California Press, 2007.

Giroux, Henry A. *The University in Chains: Confronting the Military-Industrial-Academic Complex*. Abingdon: Routledge, 2016.

Gremel, Russell P. "When Can a Policeman Use His Gun?" *Journal of Criminal Law and Criminology* 40, no. 6 (1950): 756–60.

Grenier, Clemens, and Patrick Sakdapolrak. "Translocality: Concepts, Applications and Emerging Research Perspectives." *Geography Compass* 7, no. 5 (2013): 373–84.

Hall, Stuart. "New Ethnicities." In *Stuart Hall: Critical Dialogues in Cultural Studies*, eds. David Morley and Kuan-Hsing Chen, 442–49. London: Routledge, 1996.

Hall, Stuart, Chas Critcher, Tony Jefferson, John Clarke, and Brian Roberts. *Policing the Crisis: Mugging, the State and Law and Order*. 2nd ed. London: Macmillan, 2013.

Hamilton, Tod G. *Immigration and the Remaking of Black America*. New York: Russell Sage Foundation, 2019.

Harris, Cheryl I. "Whiteness as Property." *Harvard Law Review* 106, no. 8 (1993): 1707–91.

Hartman, Saidiya V. *Lose Your Mother: A Journey along the Atlantic Slave Route*. New York: Farrar, Straus and Giroux, 2006.

———. *Scenes of Subjection: Terror, Slavery, and Self-Making in Nineteenth-Century America*. 2nd ed. New York: W. W. Norton, 2022.

Hashim, Alice Bettis. *The Fallen State: Dissonance, Dictatorship, and Death in Somalia*. Lanham, MD: University Press of America, 1997.

Hawthorne, Camilla, and Jovan Scott Lewis, eds. *The Black Geographic: Praxis, Resistance, Futurity*. Durham, NC: Duke University Press, 2023.

Holla, Abel Bennett. "Fractured Ties: Power Competition and Politics Influencing Security Strategies of Kenya and Somalia in the Horn of Africa Region." *Path of Science* 7, no. 6 (2021): 1010–15.

Huntington, Samuel P. *The Clash of Civilizations and the Remaking of World Order*. London: Penguin, 2014.

Ignatiev, Noel. *How the Irish Became White*. London: Routledge, 2015.

Ingiriis, Mohamed Haji. *The Suicidal State in Somalia: The Rise and Fall of the Siad Barre Regime, 1969–1991*. Lanham, MD: University Press of America, 2016.

———. "How Somalia Works: Mimicry and the Making of Mohamed Siad Barre's Regime in Mogadishu." *Africa Today* 63, no. 1 (2016): 57–73.

Iyare, Austine E. "Suffering and the Encounter of the Other in African Spaces." In *Handbook of African Philosophy of Difference*, ed. Elvis Imafidon, 289–99. Cham: Springer, 2020.

Jackson, Donna R. "The Carter Administration and Somalia." *Diplomatic History* 31, no. 4 (2007): 703–21.

———. *US Foreign Policy in the Horn of Africa: From Colonialism to Terrorism.* London: Routledge, 2017.

James, Joy. *Resisting State Violence: Radicalism, Gender, and Race in US Culture.* Minneapolis: University of Minnesota Press, 1997.

Kaba, Mariame, and Andrea J. Ritchie. *No More Police: A Case for Abolition.* New York: The New Press, 2022.

Kapteijns, Lidwien. *Clan Cleansing in Somalia: The Ruinous Legacy of 1991.* Philadelphia: University of Pennsylvania Press, 2013.

Kelley, Robin D. G. *Freedom Dreams: The Black Radical Imagination.* Boston: Beacon Press, 2002. Kindle edition.

Khabeer, Su'ad Abdul. *Muslim Cool: Race, Religion, and Hip Hop in the United States.* New York: NYU Press, 2016.

Klien, Stephen A. "Public Character and the Simulacrum: The Construction of the Soldier Patriot and Citizen Agency in *Black Hawk Down*." *Critical Studies in Media Communication* 22, no. 5 (2005): 427–49.

Kusow, Abdi Mohamed. "The Genesis of the Somali Civil War: A New Perspective." *Northeast African Studies* 1, no. 1 (1994): 31–46.

Lefebvre, Jeffrey Alan. *Arms for the Horn: US Security Policy in Ethiopia and Somalia, 1953–1991.* Pittsburgh: University of Pittsburgh Press, 1992.

Lewis, I. M. "The Problem of the Northern Frontier District of Kenya." *Race* 5, no. 1 (1963): 48–60.

Lindsey, Treva B. *America, Goddam: Violence, Black Women, and the Struggle for Justice.* Oakland: University of California Press, 2023.

Lipsitz, George. "The Possessive Investment in Whiteness: Racialized Social Democracy and the 'White' Problem in American Studies." *American Quarterly* 47, no. 3 (1995): 369–87.

Luibhéid, Eithne. *Entry Denied: Controlling Sexuality at the Border.* Minneapolis: University of Minnesota Press, 2002.

Mamdani, Mahmood. *Good Muslim, Bad Muslim: America, The Cold War, and the Roots of Terror.* Lagos: Malthouse Press, 2006.

Man, Simeon. *Soldiering through Empire: Race and the Making of the Decolonizing Pacific.* Oakland: University of California Press, 2018.

Maru, Mehari Taddele. "The Future of Somalia's Legal System and Its Contribution to Peace and Development." *Journal of Peacebuilding & Development* 4, no. 1 (2008): 1–15.

Mbembe, Achille. *On the Postcolony*. Berkeley: University of California Press, 2001.

McIvor, David W. *Mourning in America: Race and the Politics of Loss*. Ithaca, NY: Cornell University Press, 2016.

McKittrick, Katherine. *Demonic Grounds: Black Women and the Cartographies of Struggle*. Minneapolis: University of Minnesota Press, 2006.

Menkhaus, Ken. "US Foreign Assistance to Somalia: Phoenix from the Ashes?" *Middle East Policy* 5, no. 1 (1997): 124–49.

Mills, Andrew G., and Joseph R. Clark. "Running a Three-Legged Race: The San Diego Police Department, the Intelligence Community, and Counterterrorism." Homeland Security Policy Institute, George Washington University, HSPI brief 12, August 1, 2011. https://www.jstor.org/stable/resrep20744.

Moghaddam, Fathali M. "The Staircase to Terrorism: A Psychological Exploration." *American Psychologist* 60, no. 2 (2005): 161–69.

Mohamed, Besheer, and Jeff Diamant. "Black Muslims Account for a Fifth of All US Muslims, and about Half Are Converts to Islam." Pew Research Center, January 17, 2019. https://www.pewresearch.org/fact-tank/2019/01/17/black-muslims-account-for-a-fifth-of-all-u-s-muslims-and-about-half-are-converts-to-islam/

Montclos, Marc-Antoine Perouse de, and Peter Mwangi Kagwanja. "Refugee Camps or Cities? The Socio-Economic Dynamics of the Dadaab and Kakuma Camps in Northern Kenya." *Journal of Refugee Studies* 13, no. 2 (2000): 205–22.

Moynihan, Patrick. *The Negro Family: The Case for National Action*. Posted on BlackPast website. https://www.blackpast.org/african-american-history/moynihan-report-1965/.

Mroczkowski, Dennis P. *Restoring Hope: In Somalia with the Unified Task Force, 1992–1993*. Washington, DC: History Division, United States Marine Corps, 2005.

Muhammad, Khalil Gibran. *The Condemnation of Blackness: Race, Crime, and the Making of Modern Urban America*. Cambridge, MA: Harvard University Press, 2019.

Mummolo, Jonathan. "Militarization Fails to Enhance Police Safety or Reduce Crime but May Harm Police Reputation." *PNAS* 115, no. 37 (September 11, 2018).

Musgrave, Shawn, Tom Meagher, and Gabriel Dance. "The Pentagon Finally Details Its Weapons-for-Cops Giveaway: Bellying Up to the Arsenal." The Marshall Project, December 4, 2014. https://www.themarshallproject.org/2014/12/03/the-pentagon-finally-details-its-weapons-for-cops-giveaway.

Muslim Americans: No Signs of Growth in Alienation or Support for Extremism. Pew Research Center, report, August 30, 2011. https://www.pewresearch.org/politics/2011/08/30/muslim-americans-no-signs-of-growth-in-alienation-or-support-for-extremism/.

Newman, Graeme R., and Ronald V. Clarke, *Policing Terrorism: An Executive's Guide.* Washington, DC: Office of Community Oriented Policing Services, US Department of Justice, 2008.

Nguyen, Mimi Thi. *The Gift of Freedom: War, Debt, and Other Refugee Passages.* Durham, NC: Duke University Press, 2012.

Ododa, Harry. "Somalia's Domestic Politics and Foreign Relations since the Ogaden War of 1977–78." *Middle Eastern Studies* 21, no. 3 (1985): 285–97.

Okonofua, Benjamin Aigbe. "'I Am Blacker Than You': Theorizing Conflict between African Immigrants and African Americans in the United States." *SAGE Open* 3, no. 3 (July–September 2013).

The Other Epidemic: Fatal Police Shootings in the Time of COVID-19. ACLU Research Report, 2020. https://www.aclu.org/report/other-epidemic-fatal-police-shootings-time-covid-19.

Pierson, Emma, Camelia Simoiu, Jan Overgoor, Sam Corbett-Davies, Daniel Jenson, Amy Shoemaker, Vignesh Ramachandran, Phoebe Barghouty, Cheryl Phillips, Ravi Shroff, and Sharad Goel. "A Large-Scale Analysis of Racial Disparities in Police Stops across the United States." *Nature Human Behaviour* 4 (July 2020): 736–45.

Police Executive Research Forum. *Critical Response Technical Assessment Review: Police Accountability—Findings and National Implications of an Assessment of the San Diego Police Department.* Washington, DC: Office of Community Oriented Policing Services, 2015. https://portal.cops.usdoj.gov/resourcecenter/Home.aspx?page=detail&id=COPS-W0756.

"Police Violence against Black People Is on the Rise in Brazil." *GIGA Focus*, no. 5 (2020). https://www.giga-hamburg.de/en/publications/giga-focus/police-violence-against-black-people-is-on-the-rise-in-brazil.

Radford, Jynnah, and Phillip Connor. "Just 10 States Resettled More than Half of Recent Refugees to US." Pew Research Center, December 6, 2016. https://www.pewresearch.org/fact-tank/2016/12/06/just-10-states-resettled-more-than-half-of-recent-refugees-to-u-s/.

Ransby, Barbara. *Making All Black Lives Matter: Reimagining Freedom in the Twenty-First Century*. Oakland: University of California Press, 2018.

Rios, Victor M. *Punished: Policing the Lives of Black and Latino Boys*. New York: NYU Press, 2011.

Roberts, Dorothy E. "Race, Vagueness, and the Social Meaning of Order-Maintenance Policing." *Journal of Criminal Law and Criminology* 89, no. 3 (1999): 775–836.

Rodney, Walter. *How Europe Underdeveloped Africa*. Washington, DC: Howard University Press, 1982.

Rodriguez, Dylan. *Forced Passages: Imprisoned Radical Intellectuals and the US Prison Regime*. Minneapolis: University of Minnesota Press, 2006.

Samatar, Abdi Ismail. *Africa's First Democrats: Somalia's Aden A. Osman and Abdirazak H. Hussen*. Bloomington: Indiana University Press, 2016.

Samatar, Abdi Ismail, and Ahmed I. Samatar. "Somalis as Africa's First Democrats: Premier Abdirazak H. Hussein and President Aden A. Osman." *Bildhaan: An International Journal of Somali Studies* 2 (2002): 1–64.

Scahill, Jeremy. *Dirty Wars: The World Is a Battlefield*. London: Serpent's Tail, 2014.

Schrader, Stuart. *Badges without Borders: How Global Counterinsurgency Transformed American Policing*. Oakland: University of California Press, 2019.

Schraeder, Peter J. "The Horn of Africa: US Foreign Policy in an Altered Cold War Environment." *Middle East Journal* 46, no. 4 (1992): 571–93.

Scott, James C. *Domination and the Arts of Resistance: Hidden Transcripts*. New Haven, CT: Yale University Press, 2009.

Sexton, Jared. "People-of-Color-Blindness: Notes on the Afterlife of Slavery." *Social Text* 28, no. 2 (2010): 31–56.

Sharpe, Christina. *In the Wake: On Blackness and Being.* Durham, NC: Duke University Press, 2016.

Sheik-Abdi, Abdi. "Ideology and Leadership in Somalia." *Journal of Modern African Studies* 19, no. 1 (1981): 163–72.

Shire, Mohammed Ibrahim. *Somali President, Mohammed Siad Barre: His Life and Legacy.* Leicester: Cirfe Publications, 2011.

Shragge, Abraham J. "'I Like the Cut of Your Jib': Cultures of Accommodation between the US Navy and Citizens of San Diego, California, 1900–1951." *Journal of Sand Diego History* 48, no. 3 (Summer 2002). https://sandiegohistory.org/journal/2002/july/navy-2/.

Simpson, Gerry. "Somali Refugees in Kenya Forgotten and Abused." *The Standard.* Republished by Human Rights Watch, March 31, 2009. https://www.hrw.org/news/2009/03/31/somali-refugees-kenya-forgotten-and-abused.

———. "'Welcome to Kenya': Police Abuse of Somali Refugees." Human Rights Watch, June 17, 2010. https://www.hrw.org/report/2010/06/17/welcome-kenya/police-abuse-somali-refugees.

———. "'You are All Terrorists': Kenyan Police Abuse of Refugees in Nairobi." Human Rights Watch, March 29, 2013. https://www.hrw.org/report/2013/05/29/you-are-all-terrorists/Kenyan-police-abuse-refugees-nairobi.

Sisemore, Basima, and Elsadig Elsheikh. "The Pervasiveness of Islamophobia in the United States." Othering & Belonging Institute, University of California, Berkeley, July 21, 2022. https://belonging.berkeley.edu/pervasiveness-islamophobia-united-states.

Spillers, Hortense J. *Black, White, and in Color: Essays on American Literature and Culture.* Chicago: University of Chicago Press, 2003.

"Trusteeship Agreement for the Territory of Somaliland under Italian Administration, Adopted by the Trusteeship Council January 27, 1950." *International Organization* 4, no. 2 (1950): 347–56.

Turse, Nick. "Pentagon's Own Map of US Bases in Africa Contradicts Its Claim of 'Light' Footprint." *The Intercept,* February 27, 2020. https://theintercept.com/2020/02/27/africa-us-military-bases-africom/.

Turton, E. R. "Somali Resistance to Colonial Rule and the Development of Somali Political Activity in Kenya 1893–1960." *Journal of African History* 13, no. 1 (1972): 119–43.

UNHCR Resettlement Handbook. Geneva: UNHCR, 2011. https://www.unhcr.org/us/publications/unhcr-resettlement-handbook-and-country-chapters.

United States Department of Justice. "Investigation of the Chicago Police Department." January 13, 2017. Office of Public Affairs, US Department of Justice, "Chicago Police Department Findings." https://www.justice.gov/opa/pr/justice-department-announces-findings-investigation-chicago-police-department.

Vang, Ma. *History on the Run: Secrecy, Fugitivity, and Hmong Refugee Epistemologies*. Durham, NC: Duke University Press, 2021.

Vine, David. *The United States of War: A Global History of America's Endless Conflicts, from Columbus to the Islamic State*. Oakland: University of California Press, 2020.

Walcott, Rinaldo. *The Long Emancipation: Moving toward Black Freedom*. Durham, NC: Duke University Press, 2021.

Ware, Gilbert. "Somalia: From Trust Territory to Nation, 1950–1960." *Phylon* 26, no. 2 (1965): 173–85.

Weiss, Kenneth G. "The Soviet Involvement in the Ogaden War." Center for Naval Analyses, professional paper 269, February 1, 1980 [ADA082219]. Defense Technical Information Center. https://apps.dtic.mil/sti/citations/ADA082219.

Westad, Odd Arne. *The Global Cold War*. Cambridge: Cambridge University Press, 2006.

Wilderson III, Frank. "Gramsci's Black Marx: Whither the Slave in Civil Society?" *Social Identities* 9, no. 2 (2003): 225–40.

The World Bank. *Conflict in Somalia: Drivers and Dynamics*. The World Bank, 2005.

Wright, Michelle M. *Physics of Blackness: Beyond the Middle Passage Epistemology*. Minneapolis: University of Minnesota Press, 2015.

Zhou, Min. "Segmented Assimilation: Issues, Controversies, and Recent Research on the New Second Generation." *International Migration Review* 31, no. 4 (1997): 975–1008.

Index

abolition of police, 12, 71-72, 74-75, 98-99, 143-45. *See also* defunding of police
activism/activists: Black refugees as, 2-3; confronting anti-Black racism and militarized policing, 10-12, 71-72, 73-75, 77-79, 81-82, 83-84, 88-89, 98-99; in the global Black freedom struggle, 141-49; in the visibility of Somali refugees, 14-15; and the War on Terror, 101-3, 108-10, 111, 122, 131-32, 133-35, 136-37
Africa: Black Muslim immigration from, 12-14; the War on Terror in, 135-36, 144-45; Western imperialism in, 23-26, 29-30, 32-33, 38-39
African Americans: in media representation of American Muslims, 107-8; social media in resistance by, 79; Somali refugee solidarity with, 71-72, 74-76; War on Terror in policing of, 116-17
Afropessimism, 14-15, 77
agency of refugees, 56-57, 59-61, 62-63, 98

Aidid, Mohamed Farah, 37-38
Aidid, Safia, 26, 46
aid workers, 40-41, 61-63
Ajadi, Tari, 1
Ali, Ayaan Hirsi, 123-25
Ali, Udbi, 143
Al-Shabaab, 10-11, 102-3, 120-21, 127-28, 131-34, 136-38, 145
Amnesty International, 34, 127-28, 131, 136-37
Anti-Defamation League, 137-38
armored vehicles, 81-82, 83-85
Atanasoski, Neda, 38-39, 57-58
Atlas, Terry, 41-42
Auston, Donna, 15-16

Balko, Radley, 84
Barre, Mohamed Siad, 29-38
Berlin Conference of 1884, 23-24
Bestemen, Catherine, 32, 34, 52
Black Hawk Down (2002), 44
Black Lives Matter movement (BLM): #BlackMuslimLivesMatter, 108-9; Black Muslims in narratives of, 108-10; in confronting racism and militarized

Black Lives Matter movement
(*continued*)
  policing, 68–69, 71–72, 74–76,
    77–79, 81–83, 98–99; experiential
    knowledge of Somali refugees in,
    15–16; exposure of civilian Somali
    deaths by, 136–37; in the global
    Black freedom struggle, 141–45; in
    resisting Black death, 1–3
Blackness-as-pathology framework,
    71–72
Black Panther Party, 81
Black Twitter, 78–79, 108–9. *See also*
    social media
bodies, Black: militarized policing of,
    77–78, 80, 85, 87–88, 95–96;
    policing of, in refugee camps, 49,
    57–59; in the War on Terror, 136–37
Bogues, Anthony, 124–25
borders, 23–24, 28–29, 33, 44–45,
    118–19, 147–48
Borgen, Linda, 7
Borum, Randy, 110–11
Boutros-Ghali, Boutros, 38–39, 43–44
Browne, Simone, 82–83, 93–94
brutality of policing, 57–58, 74–76,
    77–78, 95–96, 98–99, 109

CalGang database, 92–95. *See also*
    gangs
Captain Phillips (2013), 70–71
carceral militarism: and anti-Black
    racism in San Diego, 89; and Black
    refugee subjectivity, 16–19; in the
    global Black freedom struggle,
    141–42; Islamophobia and
    terrorism studies in, 102–3; on the
    route from Somalia to San Diego,
    19–21. *See also* refugee camps

Carter, Jimmy, and administration,
    32–33, 41–42
casualties, Somali, in the War on
    Terror, 121–26, 127–33
children: in carceral refugee camps,
    55–56, 59; images of, in UN
    propaganda, 39; in kinship
    strategies, 63–64, 65–66; refugee,
    detention of, 147–48; in the War
    on Terror, 113–14, 122–23, 127–28,
    136–37
circuits of US imperialism and
    militarism, 17–18, 19–20, 69–70,
    137–38, 144, 145–46
citizenship, 54–55, 106, 114–15,
    147–48
City Heights, San Diego: anti-Black
    racism and militarized policing in,
    7–8, 9, 20–21, 69–71, 75–77, 80,
    86–89, 94–95; as carceral refugee
    camp, 66, 143–44, 147–48;
    resettlement of refugees into, 7–8,
    69–71; resistance to state violence
    in, 20–21, 91–92
civilians, Somali: executions of, by the
    Barre regime, 34; in War on Terror
    drone attacks, 126–34, 136–37
civilizing mission, 23–24, 138–39
civil war, Somali, 3–4, 17–18, 20,
    22–23, 36–43, 45–46, 86
clan system, 30–32, 36–38, 41–42,
    45–46
Clark, Joseph, 102–4, 116–17
Clarke, Ronald, 111–12
clash of civilization thesis, 125–26
Clinton, Bill, and administration,
    22–23, 138–39
Cohen, Bernard, 39
Cold War, 29–36, 38–39

collateral damage. *See* casualties, Somali, in the War on Terror
colonialism, 23-26, 27-28, 30-31, 44-45, 70-71. *See also* imperialism, US
community policing, 89-90
COPS (Community Oriented Policing Services) program, 97-98
counternarratives, Somali: in confronting anti-Black racism and militarized policing, 77, 78-79, 85-86, 95-96; on the War on Terror, 101, 102, 118-19, 131-32, 139-40
counter-policing strategies, 56-66
counterterrorism programs: Black Muslim Somali identity in, 109-11; fear of Al Shabab in rationalizing, 133-34, 137-38; globalization of, 145, 146-47; institutionalization of, 21; in militarization of police, 99, 146-47; police in, 10-11, 111-21, 145-46; secrecy in apparatuses of, 104-6; terrorism studies in justifying, 101-3, 104-6. *See also* Joint Terrorism Task Force (JTTF); War on Terror
COVID-19 pandemic, 1-2
Crawford, Neta C.: *Human Cost of the Post-9/11 Wars*, 129
criminalization of Blackness and Somali refugees: in carceral militarism, 16-17; in Dadaab refugee camp, 55-56, 65-66; in the global Black freedom struggle, 147, 148; in lived experience, 2; in militarized policing, 74-75, 76-80, 81-83, 87-88, 90-96; in policing terrorism, 112-13, 115-16; of the

refugee repertoire, 65-66; in the War on Drugs, 115-16
culture, 64, 71-72, 75, 88-89, 119, 122-24, 125
curfew laws, 66, 76-77

Dadaab refugee camp, Kenya: as carceral space, 48-50; policing in, 50-56, 143-44; refugee repertoire in, 56-67; similarity of, to City Heights, 143-44, 147-48; as a stop in resettlement, 4-7. *See also* Kenya; refugee camps
databases, 81-82, 92-95
Davis, Muriam Haleh, 14-15
defunding of police, 98-99, 144-45. *See also* abolition of police
dehumanization, 97-98, 112-13, 128-30
deportation rates for Black people, 142-43
detention/detainment, 52-53, 105-6, 118, 121-22, 142-43, 147-48
developmentalism, 26-27, 138-39
diaspora, African, 5-6, 13-14, 22-23, 74-75, 102-3, 137-38, 142-43, 144-45
dictatorship in Somalia, 1969-1990, 29-36
diversity: of origins in the US Black population, 12-13; racial, of Muslim Americans, 107-8
drones and the War on Terror, 126-39
Dudziak, Mary, 35
Dulaney, Cody, 93

equipment, military, in policing, 83-84, 99, 146, 147

Index [193]

Ethiopia. *See* Ogaden territory and war
exceptionalism, US, 138–39
experiences, lived: collective trauma in, 46–47; in creation of embodied knowledge of violence, 144–45; of the first Somali refugees in San Diego, 45; in the global Black freedom struggle, 147–48; sharing of, in surviving militarized policing, 87–89; in the War on Terror, 122

families: black, pathologizing of, 71–72; composition of, in resisting resettlement policies, 63–66; in drone attacks, 127–28, 131–32, 136–37; family networks in Dadaab refugee camp, 54–55; resources shared between in resistance, 87, 91–92; surveilling and policing of, 63–66
Fanon, Frantz, 80
Farah, Mohamed Abdihamid, 104–6
Farmer, Ashley, 81
Federal Bureau of Investigations (FBI), 10–11, 21, 110, 113–15, 118–21
Ferguson, Roderick, 13–14
Floyd, George, police murder of, 141–42, 148–49
force, police use of, 77–78, 84–85, 89, 97–99
Foucault, Michel, 64
freedom: as a Western value, in War on Terror rhetoric, 124–26, 138–39; in youth activism, 141–49

gangs, 76–77, 84–85, 92–95, 113
"General Act of the Berlin Conference on West Africa," 23–24

Ghabra, Reema, 142–43
Giroux, Henry, 103–4
Grandi, Filippo, 49
Great Britain, 24, 28–29, 51–52, 126

harassment, police, 9–10, 51, 54, 76–77, 82–83, 95–96, 98, 101–3
Hartman, Saidiya, 61–62, 72–73, 78–79
Hashin, Alice Bettis, 30–31
Hassan, Abdi, 34
Homeland Security Center of Excellence, 103–4
Homeland Security Policy Institute, 103–4
humanitarianism: in carceral refugee camps, 49, 57–58, 61, 66–67; as justification for drone attacks, 132–34; militarized, 38–43, 45–46; paternalism in, 26–27
human rights abuses, 33–34, 51–52, 53–54, 55–56
Human Rights Watch, 51–52, 54, 55–56, 121
Hussein, Abdirazak H., 29

Idd, Dola, 74, 79, 141–42
identity: Black and Muslim, 16–17, 75–76, 106–11, 112–13, 120–21, 139–40, 147; criminalization and erasure of, 16–17; in narratives of criminalization and terrorism, 147; and storytelling in the refugee repertoire, 60–61, 65; in the War on Terror, 106–11, 112–13, 120–21, 139–40
identity cards, 52–53, 66
imperialism, US: and the Barre dictatorship, 30–36; and the Black

diaspora, 13–14; carceral militarism in, 17; dehumanization of non-Western people in, 97–98; economic, 25–26; exceptionalism in legitimation of, 138–39; in the global Black freedom struggle, 144–46; in the global refugee crisis, 69–70; Muslims as perceived threat to, 120–21, 122; rise of, 23–26; and Somalian independence, 26–30; in the Somali civil war and refuge crisis, 22–23, 36–43, 44–46; in the War on Terror, 120–22, 124–25, 133–34, 135–36, 137, 138–40
information. *See* knowledge
infrapolitics, 31–32, 62–63
Ingiriis, Mohamed Haji, 31
interests, US: and the Berlin Conference, 23–24; economic, in support for the Barre dictatorship, 32–33; strategic, in imperialism, 25–26, 29–30, 32–33, 42–43, 45–46; in the War on Terror, 100
intervention, military, 3–4, 38–39, 42–43, 45–46
"Islam 101" training manual (FBI), 119–21
Islam in the War on Terror, 107–8, 119–21, 122–26
Islamophobia: and anti-Black racism, 10–11, 14–17, 100, 110–11, 139–40, 148; and Black Muslims, 109–11, 139–40; in narratives of criminality and terrorism, 147; in police militarization, 10–11; in racializing refugees as terrorist threats, 21; in terrorism studies, 100–101, 102–4; and US imperialism, 145–46; in the War on Terror, 108, 112–13, 122–26, 128–30, 138–39
Italy, 26–28

Jackson, Donna, 32–33
Jim Crow laws, 16, 148
Joint Terrorism Task Force (JTTF), 10–11, 16–17, 104, 110, 114–15, 116–17. *See also* counterterrorism programs; Federal Bureau of Investigations (FBI); San Diego Police Department (SDPD)
justice/injustice system, 76–77, 93, 113, 118

Kagnwanja, Peter, 50–51
Kapteijns, Lidwien, 35
Kelley, Robin, 142
Kenya: and British colonial government, 28–29; carceral militarism in, 17–18, 20–21; policing refugees in, 50–56, 145–46; refugee crisis in, 37–38, 46–47; refugee repertoire in, 56–66; in resettlement, 4–7; Somalians as threat in, 147–49. *See also* Dadaab refugee camp, Kenya
Khabeer, Su'ad Abdul, 14, 107–8
Kibaki, Mwai, 147–48
kinship strategies, 63–66
knowledge: in confronting militarized policing, 81–82, 88–89, 92–95; experiential, of Black Muslim refugees, 15–16; experiential, of the carceral refugee camp, 48–49; in the refugee repertoire, 55–57, 59–61, 65–66, 88–89; sharing of, in the refugee

knowledge *(continued)*
repertoire, 59–61, 65–66;
storytelling in spreading, 134–35;
in the War on Terror, 110–11, 112

language: English language skills in resettlement, 6–7; militarized, used by police, 96–98; Somali, in resistance, 88–89, 114–15; in the War on Terror, 117, 138–39
"law and order" rhetoric, 77
liberalism, Western, 111–12, 124–26
Lieberman, John, 124
Lindsey, Treva, 148
Lipsitz, George, 82–83
loitering laws, 82–83
Loria, Kevin, 97

Mahdi, Ali, 37–38, 40–41
Mamdani, Mahmood, 126
Mansoor, Sanya, 16–17
Martin, Trayvon, 73–74
Mattan, Mustafa, 108
Mbembe, Achille, 26–27
McCormick, Ty, 134–35
McKittrick, Katherine, 95–96
media, US: anti-Black racism in, 74–75, 76–77, 79; normalization of police violence by, 82–83; racialization of Somalis refugees as terrorists by, 21, 70–71, 132–34, 145–46; representation of Muslims in, 107–8, 122–25, 133–34, 136–37; representation of Somali refugees in, 5–6, 70–71; transnational and civil war in Somalia in, 36–37, 39, 41–42, 44, 45–46; War on Terror in, 129, 131–32, 133–34
militancy/militants, 116–17, 119–21

military bases: in Africa, in the global Black freedom struggle, 144–45; in militarized policing in San Diego, 8, 68–69, 83–84; secret, in Somalia, 134–36
military invasion of Somalia, 3–4, 42–44
Mills, Andrew, 102–4, 116–17
Mills, Jesse, 7–8, 143
Mohamed, Abdi, 108–9
moral panic, in the War on Terror, 115–16, 117
movement, freedom of, 2–3, 49, 52–54, 59–60, 66, 82–83
Moynihan, Patrick, 71
Mroczkowski, Dennis, 39–40
Muhammad, Khalil Gibran, 80
murder: by police, 15–16, 74–75, 77–79, 98–99, 108–9, 141–42, 148–49; of Somalis by drone, 129–30, 131–32, 136–38

National Defense Authorization Act of 2012 (NDAA), 106
Newman, Graime, 111–12
New York Police Department, 122–23
"no-knock" policies and warrants, 85–86
normalization of state violence, 77–78, 82, 121, 133–34, 136–37
Northern Frontier District, Kenya, 51–52

Ogaden territory and war, 28–29, 32–33
"Operation Restore Hope," 3–4, 16–17, 35–36, 42–44
over-policing, 10–12, 85–86

[196] INDEX

pandemics, COVID-19 and
 anti-Black racism as, 1-3
paternalism, 26-27
Patriot Act, 114-15
peacekeeping, 40-41
Perouse de Montclos, Marc-Antoine,
 50-51
poetry/poets, Somali, 46
Policing Terrorism (DOJ), 111-12
politicization of refugee youths,
 71-72, 74-76
population: of African immigrants and
 refugees, 72-73; African immigrants
 in growth and diversity of, 12-13;
 Black Muslims in, 14; of Dadaab
 refugee camp, 50-51; of Somalia,
 139-40; of Somali refugees in San
 Diego, 112-13, 139-40
poverty, 71-73, 75, 90-91
profiling, racial: in Dadaab refugee
 camp, 52; in the global Black
 freedom struggle, 145-46; in lived
 experience of Black men and
 refugees, 2; in militarized
 policing, 73-75, 82-83, 87-89,
 90-96; in the War on Terror,
 10-11, 116-17, 132-33
protection: and carceral militarism,
 49; of humanitarian aid, in the
 transnational war in Somalia,
 38-39, 40-41; in militarized
 policing, 12, 83-84; mutual, in
 refugee communities, 12, 59-60;
 of police, in the use of military
 equipment, 83-84; of property, as
 goal in the War on Terror, 111-12;
 of Somalis, in the Italian
 trusteeship, 26-27
protests, 1-2, 10-11, 74-76, 81-83

racialization of Black people as
 criminals and terrorist: Islamophobia in, 21, 101; in militarized
 policing, 70-71, 75-77, 80, 81-83,
 97-98; in the War on Terror, 104,
 111-12, 116-17, 120-21, 127-28,
 132-33, 137-38, 145-46
racism, anti-Black: and the Black
 Muslim refugee, 14-16; in carceral
 militarism, 16-17; counter-technologies in confronting, 81-83,
 92-96; in criminalization, 76-80;
 in the global Black freedom
 struggle, 142-43, 146, 147, 148; in
 inclusion in gang databases,
 92-95; and Islamophobia, 10-11,
 14-17, 100, 110-11, 139-40, 148; in
 negotiating Blackness in San
 Diego, 71-76; as pandemic, 1-3;
 and resettlement in San Diego,
 69-71; in the War on Terror,
 100-101, 104, 108-9, 110-11,
 137-38, 139-40
racism, structural, 67, 72-73, 98-99,
 108-10, 125-26, 139-40
radicalization, 21, 102-3, 110-11
Ransby, Barbara, 79
Reagan, Ronald, and administration,
 29-30, 41-42
reform, politics of, 98-99
Refugee Acts, Kenya, 52-54, 55-56
refugee camps: as carceral spaces,
 17-18, 49; as home, 48-49; living
 conditions in, 5-6; policing in,
 50-56; refugee repertoire in, 56-66;
 route to, and resettlement from,
 4-7; surveillance in, 20-21, 49, 52,
 53-54, 57, 59-60, 63, 65-66. *See also*
 Dadaab refugee camp, Kenya

Index [197]

refugee crisis, 3, 33, 37–38, 40–41, 44–46, 69–70, 132–33
refugee epistemology, Somali: and the Black Lives Matter movement, 15–16; carceral militarism in, 17–18, 49, 50–56, 59–61; in the global Black freedom struggle, 144–45; on militarism and policing, 9; in the "refugee repertoire," 60–61, 65; US imperialism in, 34, 41–42; and the War on Terror, 100, 101–2, 118–19, 122, 134–35
refugee repertoire, 5–7, 55–67, 87–89, 91–92
representations of Muslims and Somalis: paternalism in, 26–27; in popular culture, 122–25; in US imperialism, 42–43; in the US media, 5–6, 70–72, 74–75, 107–8, 122–25, 133–34, 136–37; in the War on Terror, 122–25
resettlement, 4–8, 48–49, 50–51, 52, 63–66, 69–70, 72–73
resources: in carceral refugee camps, 54–55, 61; in confronting militarized policing and racial profiling, 72–73, 87–89, 91–92; in hostility to refugees, 147–48; pooling of, in community survival, 20–21; redistribution of, from police to services, 98–99 (*See also* defunding of police); in the War on Terror, 111–12, 117, 140
Rios, Victor, 93–94
Roberts, Dorothy, 77
Rumbuat, Rubén, 7

Samatar, Abdi: *Africa's First Democrats*, 26–27

San Diego: criminalization of Blackness in, 76–80; militarized policing in, 7–12, 68–69; negotiating Blackness in, 71–76; resettlement of refugees in, 69–71
San Diego Police Department (SDPD): in criminalizing Blackness, 76–77; militarized policing by, 9–12, 68–69, 83–92, 96–98, 145; in racialization of Somalis as terrorists, 145–46; and the technologies of policing, 81–83, 92–96; use of special weapons and tactics teams by, 17–18, 83–92; use of terrorism studies by, 102–3, 104, 106; in the War on Terror, 10–11, 110–15, 116–17, 118–21, 133–34. *See also* Joint Terrorism Task Force (JTTF)
San Diego Union-Tribune, 132–34
Saunders, Mark, 83–84
Scahill, Jeremy, 121, 128
Schrader, Stuart, 146
Schraeder, Peter J., 32
scientific socialism, 30
Scott, James, 61–63
searches and search warrants, 84–86, 88–89, 97–98, 113–14
secrecy: of militarized policing, 93; in US imperialism, 122; in the War on Terror, 104–6, 131–32, 134–37
segmented assimilation theory, 71–72
Serle, Jack, 129–30
Sharia Law, 124
Sharpe, Christina, 1–2
Shih-tsung, Wang, 23–24
Shragge, Abraham, 8
slavery, 13–15, 16, 23–24, 107

social media, 78-79, 81-83, 108-9, 136-37
solidarity, Somali/African American, 71-72, 73-76, 87-89
Somalia/Somali state: British and US colonialism in, 23-26; Cold War and US-supported dictatorship in, 30-36; collapse of, in development of the refugee repertoire, 67; independence of, 26-30; population of, 139-40; sovereignty of, 23-24, 40-41, 42-43; transnational war in, 1991-present, 36-43
Somali Nationalist Movement, 37-38, 42
Somali Women's Advocacy Group, 113-14
Somali Youth League (SYL), 9, 26-30
Soviet Union, 32-33, 35, 36-37, 41-42
Spagat, Elliot, 132-33
storytelling. *See* refugee epistemology, Somali
surveillance, state: in the carceral refugee camp, 20-21, 49, 52, 53-54, 57, 59-60, 63, 65-66; crime mapping in, 94-96; in the global Black freedom struggle, 145-46; in militarized policing, 10-11, 73-74, 76-77, 79-80, 81, 87-96; in the War on Terror, 10-11, 101-3, 104-6, 112-17, 118-19, 120-22, 134-36, 139-40
SWAT teams, 68-69, 70, 83-87, 95

technology: counter-technologies, 20-21, 81-83, 92-96; in militarized policing, 92-98; in the Wars on Terror and Drugs, 10-11, 112-13, 120-21, 126-39

terrorism: in carceral militarism, 17, 18-19; equating Muslims with, 102-6, 123-26, 137-38; in militarized policing, 10-11, 89-90, 99, 145-46; policing of, 111-21; racialization of Somalis refugees as terrorists, 21, 51-52, 70-71, 132-34, 145-46; racial narratives of, in the global Black freedom struggle, 147; in refugee camp policing, 51-52, 55-56; scholarship on, 100-106. *See also* War on Terror
Terrorist Early Warning Unit (TEW), 112
Third Jihad, The: Radical Islam's Vision for America, 122-25
Thompson, Debrah, 1
traffic stops, 90-91
training manuals, law enforcement, 21, 101, 110, 119-21
translators, Somali, as informants, 114-15
tribalism. *See* clan system
Trump, Donald, and administration, 138-39, 147-48
"Trusteeship Agreement for the Territory of Somaliland under Italian Administration," 26-28
Turse, Nick, 135-36
Turton, E. R., 27-28

United Nations: invasion of Somalia by, 42-43; security forces, 40-41, 42; and Somalian independence, 26, 27; in transnational warfare in Somalia, 38-43; United Nations High Commissioner for Refugees, 52-53, 54-55, 58-59, 62-66; UN

United Nations *(continued)*
  Resolution 751, 40–41; UN
  Resolution 767, 43
United Somali Congress, 37–38, 42
United Task Force (UNITAF), 42–43
Universal Declaration of Human
  Rights, 53–54
US Africa Command, 130–31

Vang, Ma, 105–6
veterans, military, 68–69, 96–98
Vine, David: *The United States of War*,
  36–37
visibility/invisibility: of Black
  Muslims, 106–8, 122; of Blackness,
  in racism and militarized policing,
  77, 80, 82–83; of police violence,
  82–83; of Somali refugees, 14–15,
  141–42; of Somalis as Muslim and
  Black, 112–13; of state power and
  violence, in the War on Terror,
  118–19, 122, 136–37

War on Drugs: anti-Black racism and
  militarized policing in, 85, 96–97,
  99; in the global Black freedom
  struggle, 146–47; in police
  militarization, 9–10; and the War
  on Terror, 101–2, 113–14, 115–16,
  140
War on Terror: being Black and
  Muslim in, 106–11; drones in,
  126–39; in the global Black
  freedom struggle, 146–47;
  Islamophobia and racialization in,
  21; in police militarization, 9–10,
  99; policing in, 111–21; in
  rationalizing US military violence,
  121; Somali casualties in, 121–26,
  127–33; terrorism studies in,
  100–106; and the War on Drugs,
  101–2, 113–14, 115–16, 140. *See also*
  terrorism
weapons: in militarized policing,
  81–82, 83–87, 99; US supplied, in
  transnational war in Somalia,
  32–33, 41–42; in the War on Terror,
  99, 113–14, 115–16, 126–39
Wilderson, Frank B., III, 14–15, 77
world-making practices, 5–7, 12
Wright, Michelle, 13

youths, Somali refugee: and the
  Black freedom summer, 141–49; in
  confronting racism and militarized policing, 70–77, 78–83,
  85–86, 87–90, 92–94, 95–96, 98;
  counternarratives of, 77, 78–79,
  85–86, 95–96; in exposing US
  violence, 101–2, 136–37; FBI focus
  on radicalization of, 21; in racial
  justice activism, 2–3; resistance to
  police militarization by, 10–12;
  surveillance of, in carceral refugee
  camps, 66; and the War on Terror,
  101–3, 106, 108–9, 111, 113, 119–20

Founded in 1893,
UNIVERSITY OF CALIFORNIA PRESS
publishes bold, progressive books and journals
on topics in the arts, humanities, social sciences,
and natural sciences—with a focus on social
justice issues—that inspire thought and action
among readers worldwide.

The UC PRESS FOUNDATION
raises funds to uphold the press's vital role
as an independent, nonprofit publisher, and
receives philanthropic support from a wide
range of individuals and institutions—and from
committed readers like you. To learn more, visit
ucpress.edu/supportus.